THE MINDSET

THE COMPLETE GUIDE FOR TRADING SUCCESS

PREFACE

Friends, I am immensely glad to share my trading experience in the form of this book. We all are aware of how painful, disturbing, emotional and economically exhausting a trading journey can be.

This is my honest effort to help to guide all trading enthusiasts out there who are willing to make trading as a career. As trading isn't backed by any organised institutional curriculum like any other professional academic skills like medical engineer lawyer etc.

I came across many difficulties throughout my journey which I think today are very basic and stupid and cost me huge which was easily avoidable under the guidance of any mentor or book.

Hence in order to protect beginners in the trading community from early mistakes of their trading career which can become grave, serious and life threatening in many cases. I decided to write this book on the basis of my own experience.

Trading journey for most of the people remains so hard full of chaos with tonnes of confusion and biases. This is my sincere efforts to help those throughout the journey in order to reduce damage to their economical and mental health.

Well begun is half done friends hence start your trading journey under guidance of this book with proper mindset at first place that will certainly reduce your hustle and make you successful profitable trader without much time and cost damage.

I don't want this book to be just a storytelling one like many others in the market but to give you a clear cut concept of trading psychology which contributes 90% for trading subjects. Which I noticed from my hard core experience.

Also I have provided substantial information about technical analysis as well in a short and crisp manner which will certainly be useful to you guys.

I have made my important image base notes which I found very useful to remember core concepts of trading that I have shared in this book. I went through immense struggle during my decade-long journey.

So much time was wasted of mine due to ignorance before coming to the right direction of learning. Hence I wanted to share whatever knowledge I have gathered to the people to help them with whatever I have.

I clearly witnessess the lack of books regarding this subject. There is a big gap of academic book benefits in this field so this is my small attempt for the fulfilment of this same gap.

I have shared my own approach towards charting my own strategy for Intraday trading which I found useful after a long hustle.

You guys can benefit from it if you find it relevant according to your observation as well. All your suggestions and feedback will be appreciated.

Experience, exposure, learning, screwing, absorbing and eventually implementation all that is going to take time.

Hence start your journey with the virtue of patience and trust in the process. All your hard work will pay off for sure.

All the best.

AUTHOR

DR. ASHISH MASRAM

CONTENTS

Chapter 1

RIGHT APPROACH ATTITUDE AND ATTRIBUTES

Learning is a process. Process means time taken mechanism. This is the basic principle of learning. To learn anything new we need to know its subject content context.

We can't learn anything at one point of time. We aren't machines, we are human. We need a period of time to know, to learn, acquire and apply.

This simple basic mindset preparedness can prevent hurry and impulsion mediated damage during our journey. Ideal learning approach required considering trading is altogether a different world.

We simply can not conclude anything out of it within a short period of time with potential lack of information.

This kind of approach can reduce our economical expectations from the market and focus our mind on the learning aspect of it. Friends do remember the mindset is the key to success here from day one to throughout your journey.

Hence I'm putting more emphasis on it at the very start of your journey. Mindset preparedness is the first step not the last one. We need to understand this.

Reckless and egoistic attitude is the soil for destruction. Prevention is better than cure. Learning time is better than repairing time. All the efforts should be made to do least damage in order to reduce our loss recovery period after substantial learning occurs.

PATIENCE , discipline, control, stillness of mind , less expectations, learning, preparation, evaluation every now and then are the key attributes required for trading.

MINDSET preparedness should occur prior to entry into the trading world. As we go through any academic curriculum. Where we learn theory first prior to entering or performing practical.

It's a serious business with an involvement of potential huge risk. Prior analysis of own requirement expectations from the trading must be fixed.

Trading is an ocean of opportunities. But we need to start gradually and cautiously. Need to check our thoughts , actions, doing, predilections , contradiction mental and technical both every now and then.

Sincerity, consistency and right work for the right amount of time are absolutely necessary. If you are among non serious candidates throughout life and you keep the same mindset here you might invite big trouble for you.

STEPS TO BE FOLLOW

STEP 1 - Knowing technical fundamentals concept in trading and apply it in small quantities with a higher time frame initially.

STEP 2 - Writing a journal knowing doing our own mental analysis.

STEP 3 - After gathering some sort of experience of delivery short term trading one can move to INTRADAY trading IN EQUITY.

STEP 4 - DERIVATIVE (FUTURE OPTIONS) Must be done after a good amount of experience in the market and after having good technical analysis skill. Otherwise this could be a disastrous decision in many cases.

I made the same mistake by entering directly into the derivative segment without any proper information and technical skill. That cost me a lot. So better you guys proceed gradually with the incremental order of volatility with advancement of your technical knowledge.

But unfortunately nothing sequential happened in real life. Most of us directly enter In the derivative intraday trading and suffer a lot due to emotional havoc produced owing to abrupt volatility in the market. Hence the first thing first must be done. This book is for the same to guide you in appropriate manner from where to start, how to start when to climb.

DONT WASTE TIME MONEY ENERGY BEHIND RANDOM OUTCOME IN MARKET BY INDULGING IN CARRY FORWARD AND HERO ZERO. CONSISTENCY CAN BEAT ANY SUCH RANDOM POSSSIBILITIES WITH PEACE OF MIND AND QUALITY TRADING.

REMEMBER LESS IS MORE HERE.

GROW GRADUALLY ITS AN ART AND SCIENCE IN NATURE. SO ITS TRUE FOR TRADING AS WELL. SO STAY SOMEWHAT DISTANT DETACHED TO OBSERVE AND APPLY WELL. LEARNED GREAT PARADOX IN LIFE HURRY MEANS LATE. PATIENCE IS PROCESS OF CULTIVATION. IT CONSIST GREAT HIDDEN MAGIC.

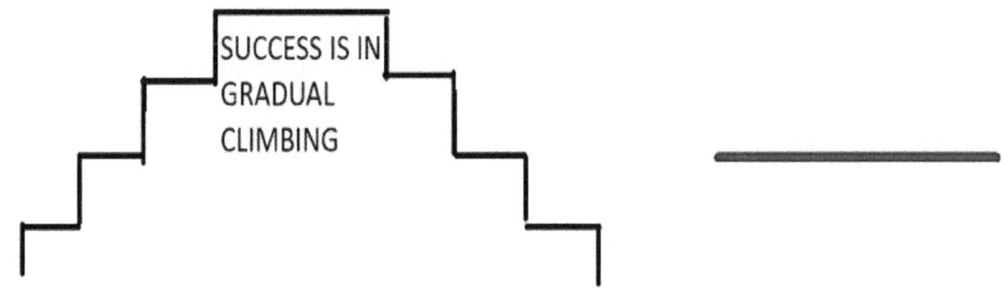

Learning that hurry means delay is an important aspect in trading.

Turtle approach required in the trading.

We suppose to mentally prepare ourselves that it's going to take time to acquire a proper mindset skillset in this field.

When we drive a car from an area where visibility is impaired due to environmental factors. What we do in that case. We drive it slowly gradually till things get clearer to visible.

Same sort of gradual steady going approach required with experimenting with our new learning before reaching our final interpretation.

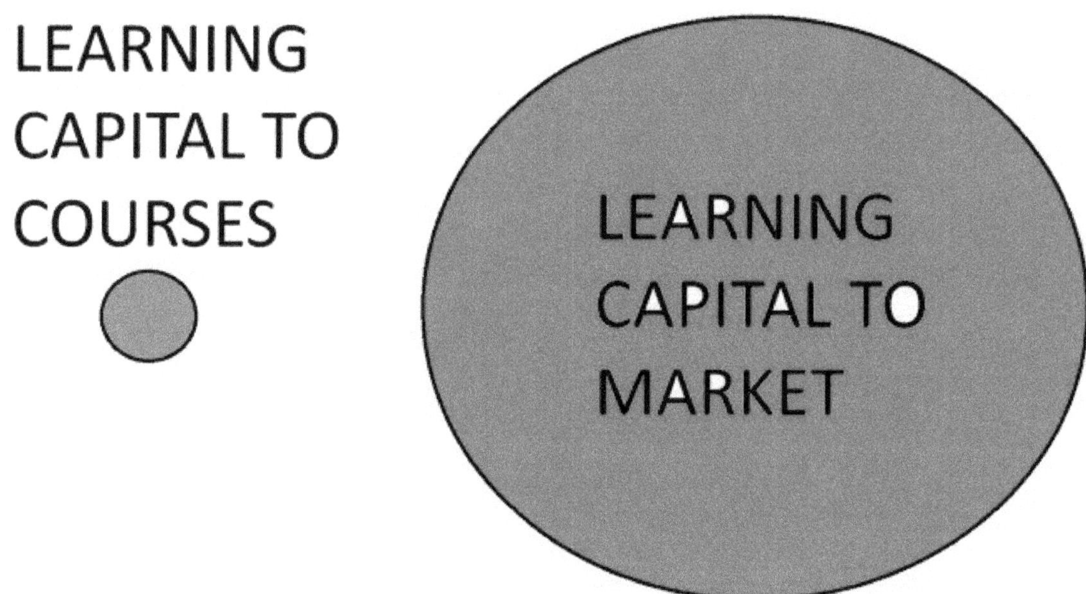

Guys dont forget that you are new in the trading world. You hardly know anything about the market . How it functions. Who are the key participants here? You probably don't know how to place orders as well. Hence better to take some courses and add some orientation in your mind.

Certainly courses alone are not going to make you profitable , your own experience will. But by taking courses you will certainly get a fair amount of ideas where we shouldn't waste our money.

Cost you pay for the courses will certainly be lower than if you tried alone to figure out the market without taking any help during your initial years.

Don't we take courses to learn anything in this world? Guidance mentorship is always necessary in every field at least in the beginning before we conquer our own way out.

DISCIPLINE ORIENTED APPROACH

IS THE KEY TO SUCCESS

NOT MONEY MAKING APPROACH

USE YOUR PRICE ACTION KNOWLEDGE TO CHOOSE PRODUCTIVE TRADE WISELY.

Don't run behind money. Run behind the figure out process which suits you most. That's why a journey is required. You need to develop your price action knowledge over the period of time to bring proximity with the chart with the market along with its trends and gyration.

What is trade, what does it consist of? Trade is movement of underline instruments along desired anticipated direction.

For that we require 3 points

3 key levels

1) Entry level.
2) Stop loss level
3) Target level.

Stop loss is our friend throughout the journey for sustainability .

Longer we survive here high chances of becoming among successful profitable traders.

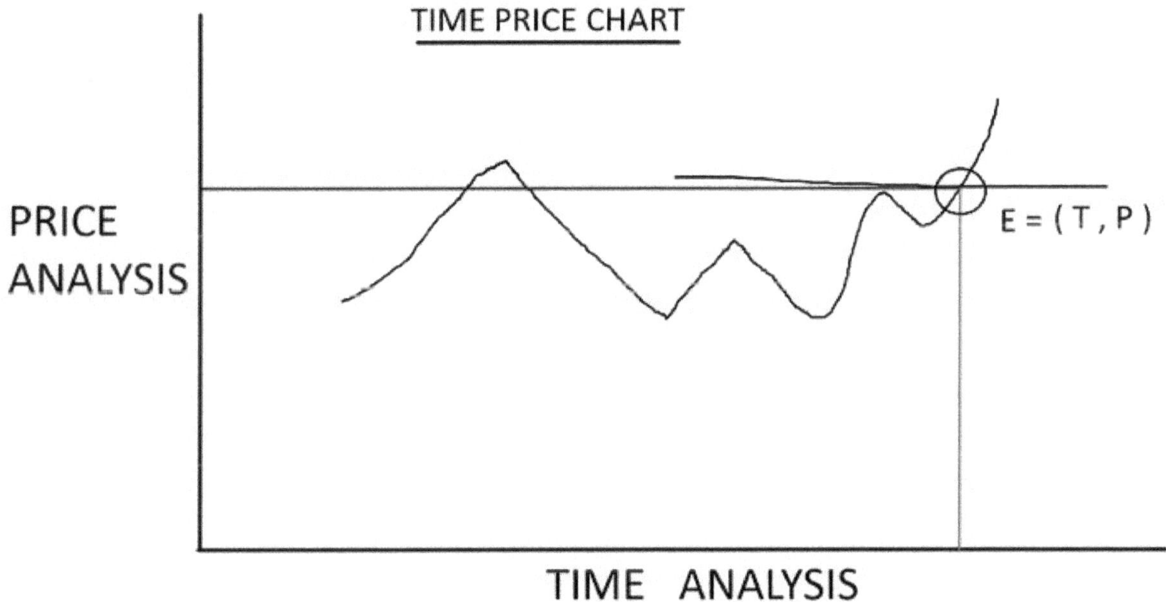

E= Entry point.

Chapter 2

PRIMITIVE BEHAVIOUR

We all are animals. Yes we were born and evolved out of it. We are full of primitive animalistic instincts. We are inherently violent, commanding, dominating and controlling in nature. Probably to obtain better security in the primitive era.

This very animalistic nature of ours leads to severe damage in our trading journey. Rather than understanding the market we try to control it. And problems start then after. To become a good trader we don't need to control the market but to understand it in totality with its participants' constituents mechanism of action.

One human or group of humans can't control the market. It's huge to handle any one singular opinion. Hence both side preparedness, watchfulness and adaptation flexibility are of more importance than rigid one side bias.

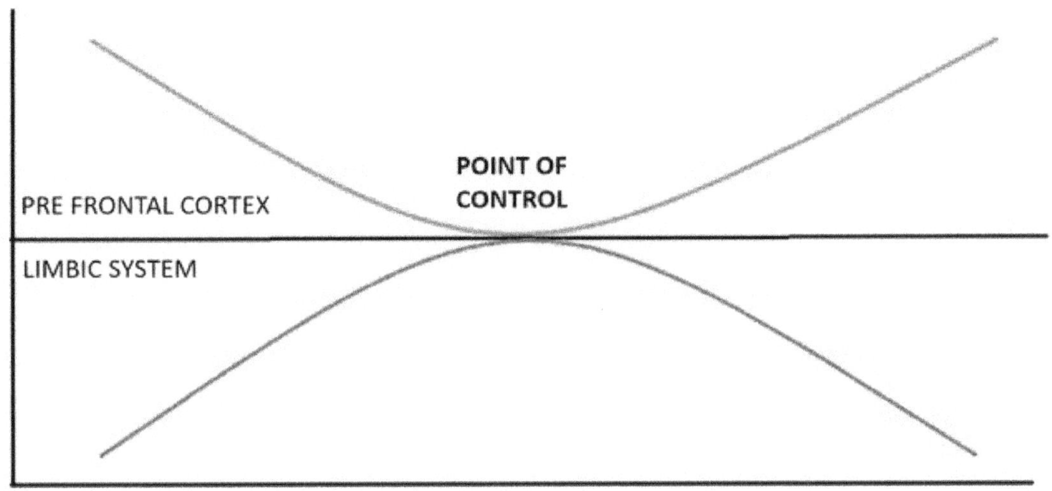

GRAPH SHOWING EVOLUTION OF TRADER BRAIN

Trading minds need to be evolved, dear friends. Nobody was born as a trader. And humans are certainly not born for it. Trading is inherently against our natural instinct. Hence probably a difficult skill to pursue. Market is vast in terms of its participants' constituents, instruments and behavioural variation. Good information alone is not good enough to conquer. Many times we aren't able to act upon whatever market information in front of us.

We not only react opposite to it but are unable to change direction despite having heavy losses in front of our eyes. Market is simple in its presence. Apparently trading seems easy in terms of taking only buy and sell decisions.

But it's not that easy in the real world due to our very emotional complexity in this business rather than objectivity. It took years to develop some common sense in trading.

Yes friend, common sense is good enough to become a successful trader . But we completely lack it in the initial year. Our mind takes much more time than we thought to connect all the dots of our journey. And make us reach at the level of what we call trading mindset.

This is the journey of uncontrollable emotional behaviour of ours in the market due to the limbic system to the time being acquiring skills where we can take experience base database objective decisions over charts .

Journey of obtaining control over our mind in order to make rational logical decisions in the market.

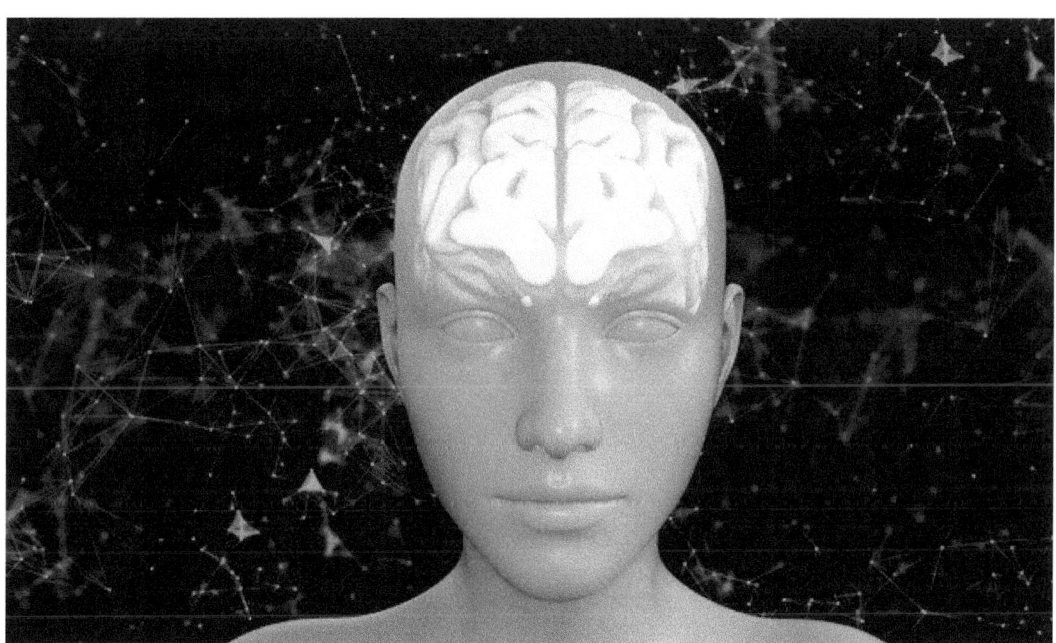

STRUGGLE TO OBTAIN CONTROL OVER MIND.

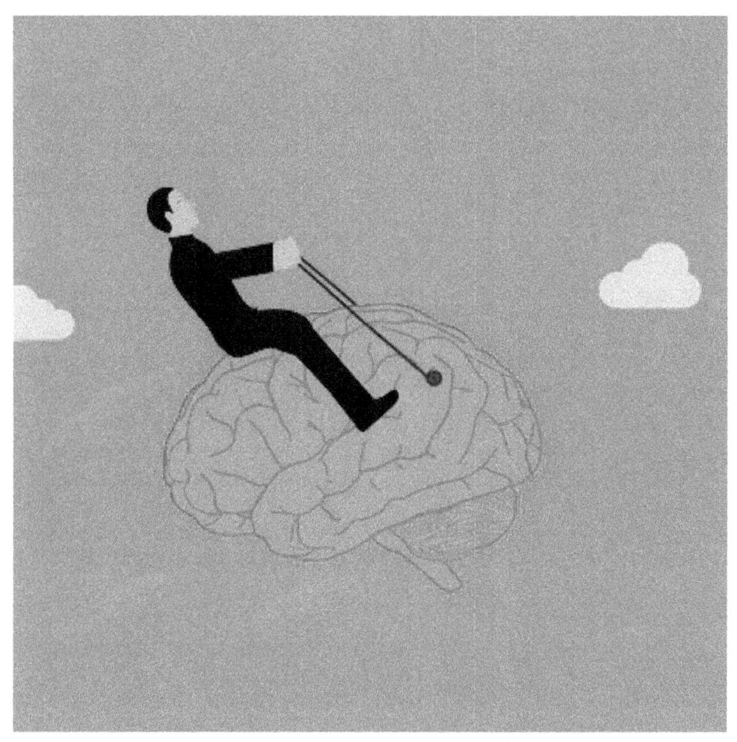

Chapter 3

EXPECTATIONS MANIA

You know nothing about trading and the market and you expect everything from it from day one. How does this sound? But yes this is the reality of every trader. From where the hell this kind of thought urges compulsion superiority complexes comes in the mind.

This book is about that. The quest the enquiry about it. The inquest to know why 90% traders failed in the stock market and only 10 % made profit. Despite such organised digital availability of it with a lot of resources research information tools technical strategy.

Problems must lie beneath our core. How and why we behave in such idiotic manner in this field. Despite this, we have conquered almost everything on this planet in terms of understanding knowledge whatever.

Long term horizon necessary to expect some significant outcome from this field. Probably a time approach could be best to sustain survival and growing. Trading is not a quick rich scheme. It doesn't work like that.

It is going to take multiple years to prepare that trading mindset which will make you in the 5 to 10 % club of significant profitable traders.

Hence don't look for a return from day one. Look for things which are supposed to be learned in the market. Technical analysis, fundamental analysis and own analysis as well.

Statistics have clearly shown that very few people are able to make money in the market. In Intraday trading the number is again small. Despite this well known statistical truth we consider ourselves a special entity and try to become millionaires within a couple of years of our trading career.

This kind hypothetical expectation only leads to delayed learning and deterioration of mental, emotional and economical health.

Do we make money just by joining any professional school, medical engineer or lawyer?

We need to complete its academic course then need to do an internship to gain experience of its practical implementation.

After a good amount of preparation and experience we started to earn some bucks.

HUMAN GREED

But in trading we want to earn more than any profession from day one. We completely ignore the learning aspect of trading. Probably due to how trading appears easy just doing buy and sell.

But there is a whole lot of technical fundamental psychological analysis behind that decision. Learning aspect of trading is hidden; it's not apparently well documented and organised back up by institutions.

Above all we humans by default are not prepared to work in a nonlinear environment like trading.

Nowadays we all are victims of instant gratification. We can't wait for long term preparation for delayed gratification.

Delayed gratification has significant importance in trading . Marathon runner required.

Chapter 4

UNKNOWN TERRITORY

Have you ever thought of going travelling to some distinct place? Most of us for sure. Then how we planned our trip. With all kinds of detailing. Right from tooth brushes to T-shirts.

We never mess up on those occasions. We planned it with all our wisdom, intelligence and available resources. But what happened in share market trading. Do we plan? Do we ever think of it? Or we just run to make money. Despite having no clue or knowledge of making it.

How to handle and approach the unknown with consciously this common sense does lack in many people in this journey. And that is bound to create trouble.

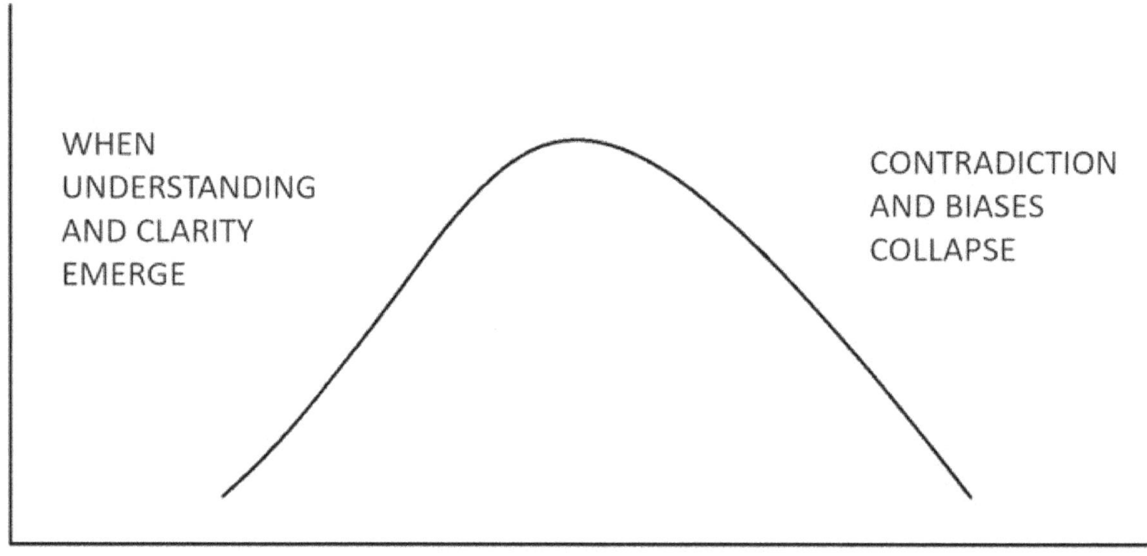

We encounter tremendous contradictions in this field when we enter. You can participate in the market in many ways.

Short term long term or on Intraday basis. We went through a hell lot of confusion during the initial year: what instrument we were supposed to choose to play for what time frame, which strategy breakout, pullback reversal or anything else.

Which indicator to choose? Many times they are contradictory also. In market changing dynamics some strategies work some not. What suits where the answer will be given by experience only.

With the experience of market trends sentiment you will be able to choose appropriate strategy tools according to scenario. Till then it's going to be hell.

It's a journey of knowing your own darkness and illuminating yourself with self knowledge to become successful.

Experience can lead us to perform linear fashion in non linear entities also . The human mind has that capacity. We just need to give time and organise our learning in every field.

Chapter 5

SYMPATHETICOVERDRIVE

We humans are distinct from other animal species mostly due to our evolved nervous system. Which is broadly classified as central and peripheral. In which peripheral further get classified in Autonomic nervous system and somatic.

Autonomic nervous systems further classified into Sympathetic is fight and flight response and parasympathetic rest and digest.

TheSYMPATHETICcomponentofourANSsystembringsalotofhell in our trading journey due to its relationship with fight and flight response to unknown subjects.

Till we understand core concepts of trading which are suitable to us, our evolved nervous system keeps fighting with ourselves with lots of emotional and economical damages.

The prevention mechanism once a while in our primitive era became our most profound hurdles and stumble blocks in our trading journey.

To solve the problem we first must know the problem in detail. Every trader must know from where their impulsive reckless trading behaviour comes to overcome it.

Ask yourself if you are desperate to make money. Have you gathered all the essential information about trading?

Have you accomplished technical and emotional prerequisites before expecting anything in return out of it. Have you become familiar enough with charts?

Have you experienced a market with logic in all possible trends? Does your concept are logical in accordance with the current scenario in the market?

Ask these questions to bring some proximity with the market before expecting and indulging ourselves with a market with big money and big risk for big returns.

If the answer is no you are likely to end up in huge losses due to triggering this sympathetic overdrive to the unknown. Be aware of it.

GRADUAL

THOUGHT PROCESS

LOGIC CONCEPT

CONTEXT CLARITY

CONTROLLED

IMPLEMENTATION WITH

EXPERIENCE AND

KNOWLEDGE

CLIMBING

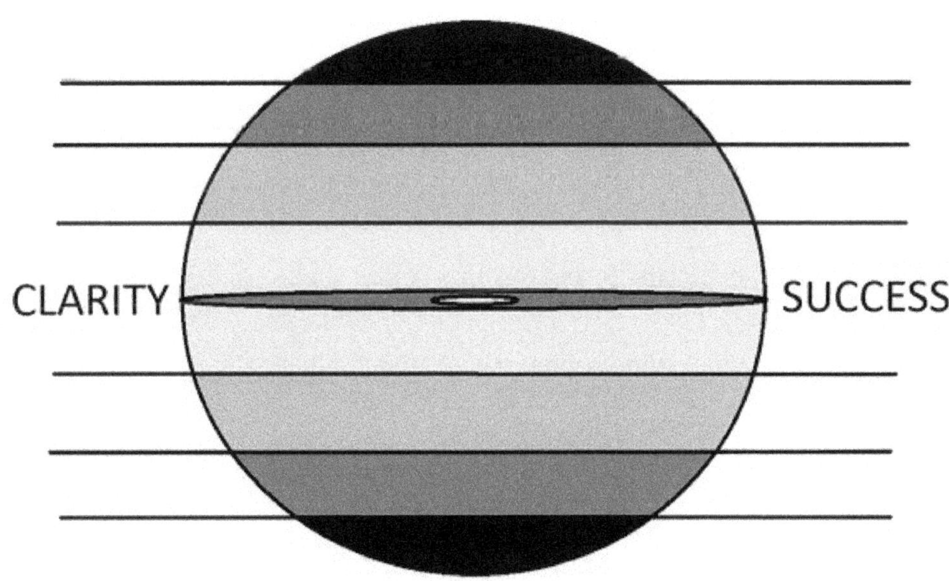

360 DEGREE ALL ROUND EFFORTS REQUIRED TO GET THERE

Chapter 6

BIOLOGY BEHIND BEHAVIOUR

Survival Instinct. Nature gives it for our existence. We tend to move far from the object which is coming towards you in anticipation of its danger. To protect ourselves we go far from it. This survival instinct in a dangerous scenario likely contributes to our behaviour where we tend to play against the trend in the market. Considering the market is a fearful object which is coming towards us so let's go far from it.

If it moves up our natural tendency leads us to play on the downside. If it goes down our natural tendency contributes to playing us on upside. Whole lot of traders suffer due to this mental gallop. We need to understand the science behind it and conquer it.

Identification of trends on the chart with multiple time frame analysis is an important key to pick the right direction in the market. You make profit when you are in the right direction. But you won't get that ability mindset soon. Because naturally we aren't built to do so.

Playing against the trend is one of the common reasons why many traders lose horribly. They find it difficult to adapt their thoughts and predilections with the market. Don't forget the market is supreme. You have understood it.

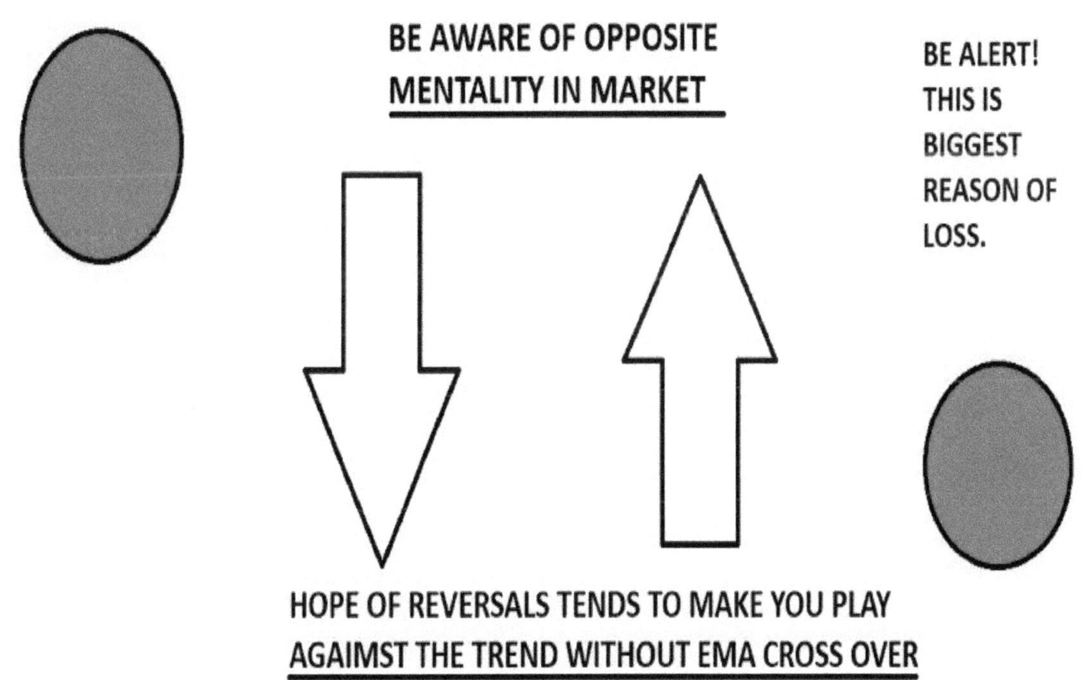

Direction is more important in trading than your speed of increasing quantity. First try to get aligned with market direction. Your predilection can create hurdles to get aligned with market direction.

If you have a presumption bias towards down side or upside you can get mentally trapped to make logical decisions in the market. And hence you may encounter several losses .

Remember we have to follow the market, not control or move it in our favourable direction. Due to primitive ego revenge trading we keep playing against the direction of the market despite witnessing several losses.

We lose the common sense that if we change and place our position according to market direction only then we can make profit. Also we are naturally incapable of taking losses.

Any sort of loss can trigger an uncontrollable panic reaction in the market. That further poised us to make several losses rather than stopping and acknowledging our mistakes. We keep making the same mistake over and over again. Animals within us don't want to listen and calm down and improve.

Trading can make you self destructive specially Intraday trading due to the addictive potential of it. Hence take a gap every now and then to do introspection of our own behaviour and maintain a trading journal for the same. Know the logical reason behind your trade . Make sure your trades are objectively aligned with the chart.

That much precaution you must take. Forget your assumption. Try to develop as much logic, concept, context as possible to make odds in your favour. Nothing 100 % sure here. But certainly you can pick high probability trades.

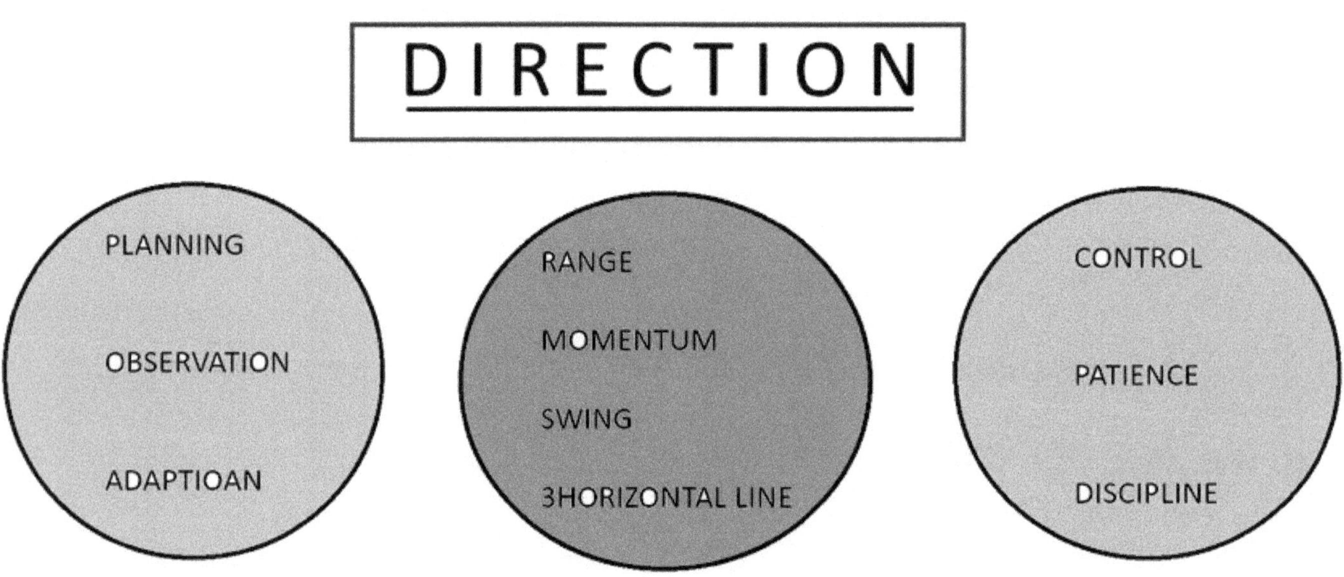

It's all about predicting, observing and being in the right direction in the trade to make money.

Keeping yourself in the right direction in the trading is the biggest challenge in the trading . Despite seeing clearly visible market direction we may not remain or take the right direction due to our premature assumption of direction and range.

This is the biggest emotional block in trading. God knows why we play opposite to market behaviour and encounter hell lot of losses even by seeing ourselves wrong in the trade on the screen.

We must know our swing cut off level, a level from which we can change our direction from up to down or down to up in order to protect our losses.

stress
fear
depression
sadness
despair

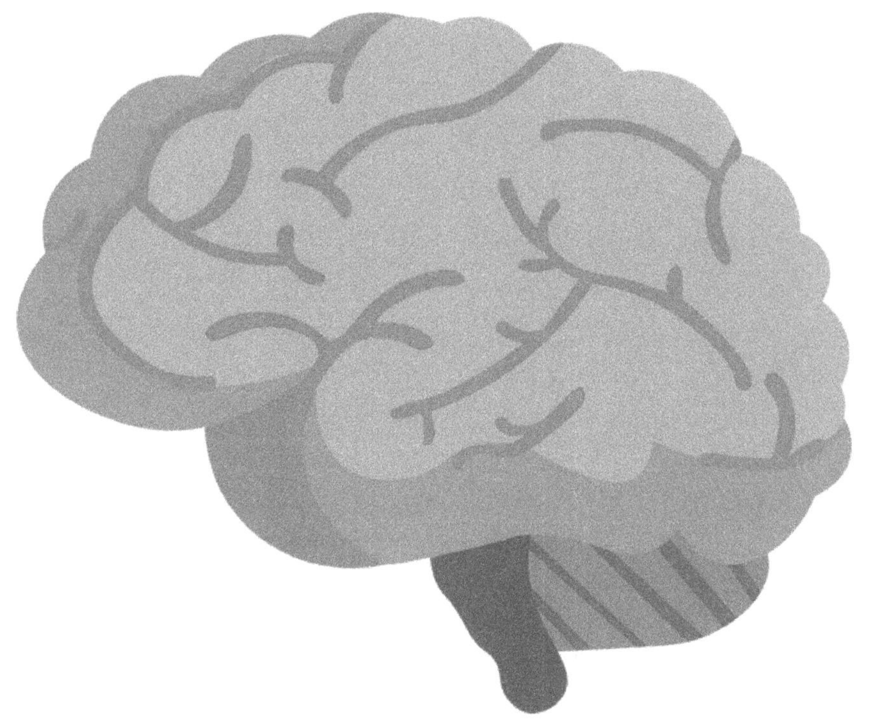

Chapter 7

TIME EXPERIENCE MATTERS

What's the treatment of phobias? Exposure exposure and more exposure. Everything is bound to get settled with time.

Thanks to God. In Nature everything is bound to get settled with time. This law of nature is the way of success during the journey of trading tunnels.

No matter how talented you are. Market is so dynamic it has so many facets you can't understand or get aware of , at any point in time. Just by knowing you can't implement and earn.

Nature doesn't give that permission. We need to challenge our Nature, we need to change ourselves to become successful traders. We need to explore not only the market but ourselves also.

Better Trader journey also makes you a better person. Because no option
left to become profitable is the only way out.

Experience has no replacement in trading that comes with the time spending only. Your familiarity, proximity and all weather exposure makes you capable enough to figure out your way of profitability.

You can be profitable with your own style.

ALWAYS HEAD FOR 15 MT 5MT SYNCHRONISATION AND BETTER RISK REWARD TRADE EVERY DAY AND OUT. DONT GET RUSH HURRY OR EXCITED WHILE TRADING.

UNDERSTAND MARKET STRUCTURE WHETHER UPTREND DOWNTREND OR CONSOLIDATION. ACCORDING TO IT PLAN BREAKOUT PULLBACK OR REVERSALS.

TRADING INCOME IS OUTCOME OF YEARS OF LONG DISCIPLINE EFFORTS. HAVE A LONG TERM HORIZON AS POSSIBLE AS.

UNDERSTAND LOGIC CONCEPT BEHIND YOUR APPROACH AND CHOOSE RELEVANT VERSION OF IT.

Maturity comes with the experience only. Our inner core gets disturbed with the market momentum and potential of it making money out of it.

We move like a pendulum according to market movement. Unless we become still inside we can't observe market movement with a keen mind to organise it to form any concept to play out in a logical manner.

Inner stillness is more important that probably comes with time spending in this field only.

Chapter 8

UNDERSTANDING EMOTIONS

Needless to say we humans are full of emotions, in fact we are fools because of emotions. We can experience throughout our trading journey.

From where these emotions are generated which creates immense hurdles in learning trading and implementing it. The answer is the limbic system in the brain. Yes this area which is a small part of our primitive brain responsible for over hyper emotional mediated response in our journey.

What not emotions we encounter while trading. Whether it's fear, greed, hope , FOMO revenge anger frustration anxiety endless list. Every dot is connected; here you elicit one emotion and it triggers many.

My purpose is not just to enumerate problems here but also provide solutions to them.

Let's think first thing first. How this emotional cycle triggers. Probably the most right answer is Greed. Undue expectations from the subject about which we are hardly aware of. Most traders started their journey as landing in unknown territory.

But human greed and their respective superiority complex which make them conclude everything in hustle and reckless manner create all kinds of emotional chaos.

We are vulnerable to play with an emotional mind due to market volatility and likely to do multiple random entries and do lots of losses.

We are supposed to protect our capital first rather than indulging ourselves in random market volatility. Don't meet the accidental loss .

Avoiding unnecessary loss is one of the major secrets of making money in the market. Instead making more money focusing on reducing losses can bring a big jump in your profit loss statement. Observe it. Any kind of random move elicits greed within us.

Hence avoiding potential volatility is one of the keys to success here. Don't get trapped by greed within you.

AVOID VOLATILITY FIRST. STOP WASTING TOO MUCH POINTS. TRADE SWING COP PAUSES. PROTECTING LOSS IS MORE IMPORTANT THAN MAKING PROFIT. WITH ONLY 2 TRADE POLICY MONEY AND POINT MANAGMENT POSSIBLE. LESS TRADE MORE PROFIT. ACCEPT IT.

We all know mindset is the key to success in trading. What if we enter in trading with the proper mindset in the first place. Rather generating a mindset after making severe losses damages to our life peace isn't it wise to enter with proper mindset from day one.

Our hurry and desperation to make money and to prove ourselves to our peers around us tends to make absurd decisions. This kind of mindset forms the soil for deterioration.

Before heading towards any technical fundamental strategic analysis of the market one must prior acquire a good stable peaceful gradual disciplined realistic mindset. This is gonna help not only in trading but also for life.

Because one who entered in trading high chances of his or her to remain in this field throughout their lives. Hence a rational pragmatic approach is key to success here.

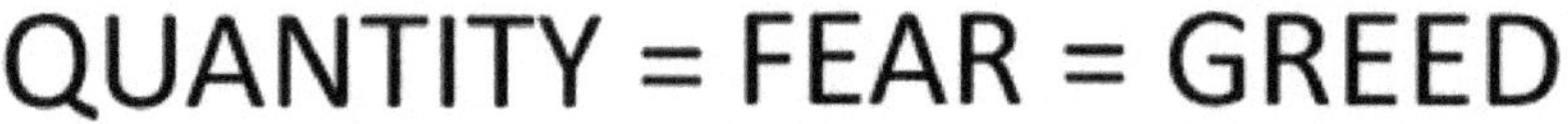

FIXED RISK REWARD

FOMO REGRET SCALPING OVERTRADING

FEAR DUE TO PROFIT DEPLETION. NO GOOD TRADE ENTRY

One of the major triggers of the vicious cycle of emotional and economical deterioration in the market is the undue quantity in comparison of our experience and knowledge, preparation.

In that case quantity can surely backfire with our trading performance. It's very obvious that with small quantities we are likely to have small losses in case we are wrong and if quantity is big loss will be big in proportion to it.

When our concept logic context over chart is ill prepared we are likely to fear price fluctuations in the market. That can trigger panic reactions in us.

We may exit prematurely to book small profit or may end up in big loss due to our inability to exit in a loss case scenario.

Instead increasing quantity we should focus on better entry points from where we have a high probability of better target. Control your greed. Quantity doesn't increase profit unless you are in the right direction in the market. First get profitable in small quantities with wisely chosen your own method.

CONSISTENCY POSSIBLE BECAUSE

1) TRADING IS LOGICAL BUSINESS. NOT GAMBLE FOR SURE.
2) OBJECTIVITY CLARITY AVAILABLE HENCE REPEATATION TOO.
3) REPEATABLE PATTERN HENCE CONSISTENCY POSSIBLE IN IT.
4) PROBLEM LIES IN INADEQUATE INPUT MISCONCEPTION MISINTERPRETATION AND ABOVE ALL GREEDY HUMAN MIND.
5) PERCENTAGE AND RATIOS MAKE YOU PROFITABLE.
6) PATIENCE AND CONFIDENCE AFTER CLARITY ARE KEYS.
7) LOGIC OBJECTIVITY MATH WITH ADDED EXPERINCE.
8) TRADING MINDSET IS ASSET. MINDSET IS EVERYTHING.

Trading is the business of logic concept context over Market. Not of the business of emotions. This we need to imbibe in our mind very deeply.

Though the market is random nothing is 100 % sure but with the experience and proper knowledge we can fairly predict and understand market gyration.

If that is not the case it's unlikely to make profit to any human on this planet.

Repetition of pattern , scenario , trends is always there; we just need to understand with our overall analysis what's the case today. That can be done with regular following markets for years and years.

It's a time consuming journey. But unfortunately most traders make it a money consuming journey as well. Due to our inability to control over greed, revenge, hope, fomo before our real time to come.

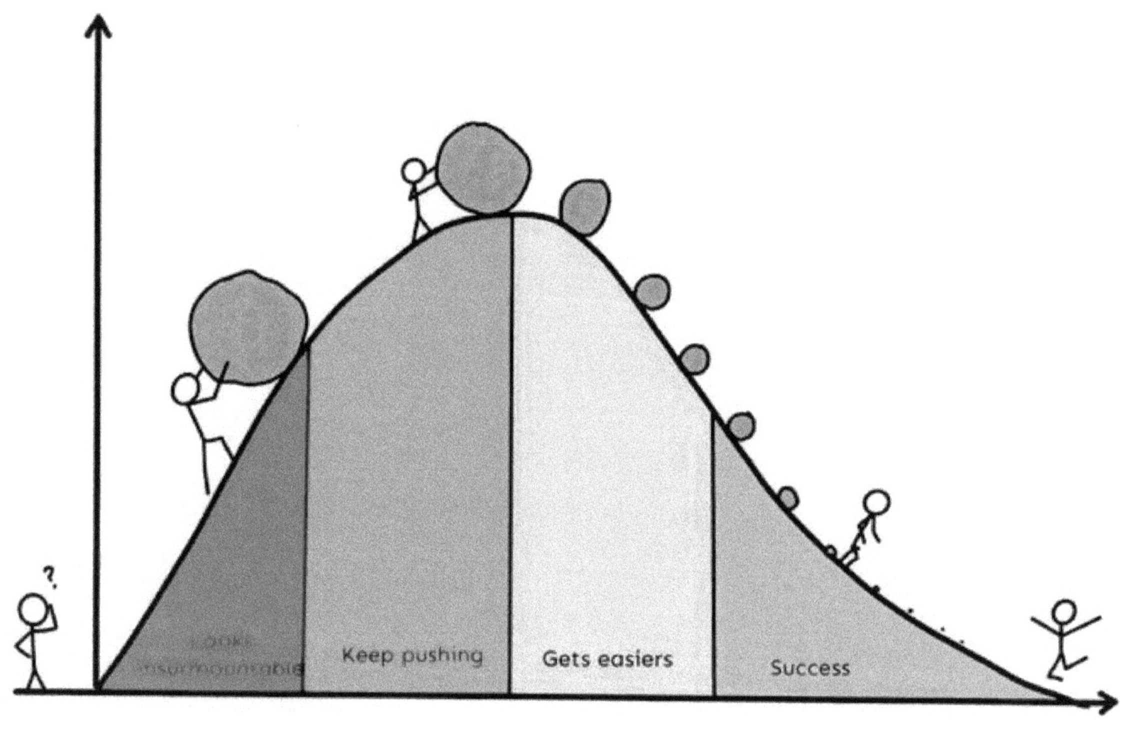
?
Looks insurmountable
Keep pushing
Gets easiers
Success

Chapter 9

THE WORLD OF MISCONCEPTION AND MISINTERPRETATION

Yes. It's an entirely different world altogether from which we used to live. The concept logic context is not linear. They are dynamic changeable according to market mood cycle behaviour patterns.

You can't draw one single conclusion and rely upon it throughout life. It's not about our misinterpretation of the market but also about ourselves.

How we humans can process and understand such a vast market to conclude it one simple logic or in one single statement.

When we enter any new field we come with a lack of information. As many traders started their journey in the market like in unknown territory information came towards them with a very unorganised scattered manner.

And as we all know half knowledge is dangerous to health. Same kind of phenomenon occurs for years and years till we finally reach something which suits our taste.

Market is a multifaceted entity that suits you; it probably doesn't suit me and vice versa. Hence probably at every point of time and price traders get divided

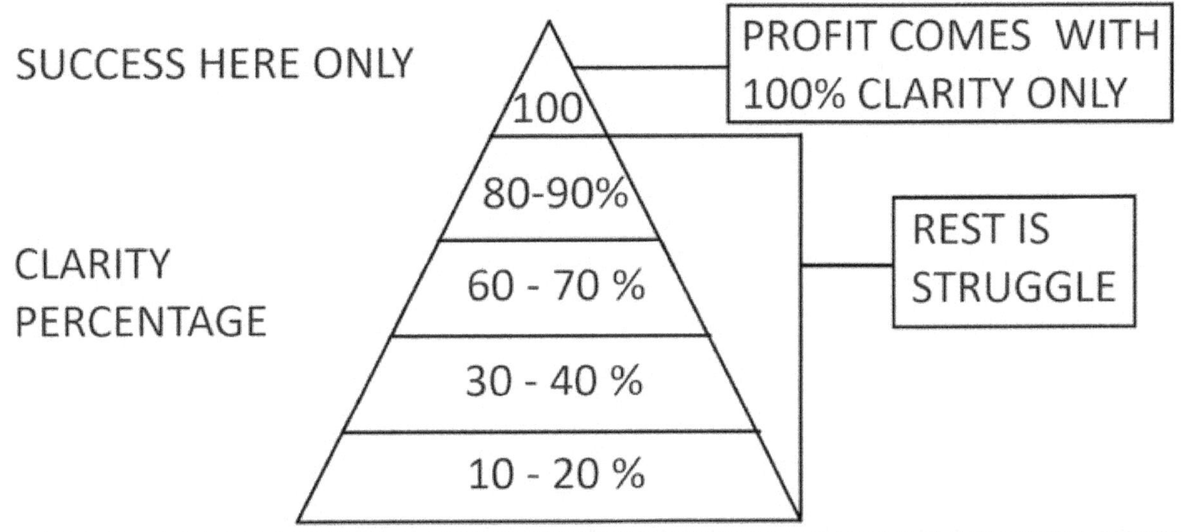

in two opinions either up and down. No single answer exists which is applicable favourable to all. Because as a rule. One has to lose in order to win against one another.

Clarity is the key to success. Clarity of our own work approach method in the market. Because clarity leads to simplicity. And simplicity leads to our ability of implementation.

When did you have clarity in the trading? During your early years of exposures. Or when you get a good amount of experience and knowledge which you have tested and observed first hand.

Certainly it's going to be a journey with multiple ups and downs. But trusting the process despite multiple failures in your journey is the only way out.

One day all the dots of your journey will get synchronised and you will be able to make money on your own without asking anybody or getting influenced by external voices.

External voices are the major culprit of our delayed interpretation of the market. But we have no option other than listening to our professional seniors till we figure out our own way.

No common answer in trading. Trading is a multifaceted entity. We have to choose our own aspect of it. Work hard to obtain your own clarity.

Trading problems are more about our behaviour problems. We need to follow this checklist before making any trade.

Ask yourself the following questions before entering in the trade that will help you keep your mind at the right place.

Try to be a grounded centred person who is not rigid about his views. He is available to adjust himself in market changing dynamics .

Though he has own analysis, his goal is to penetrate market reality . He wants to be right in the market, not in his own analysis only.

This is the difference between profitable and non profitable traders. Profitable traders always want to be right in the market, not right in their own analysis.

BEHAVIOURAL CHECK LIST

1) MAKE SURE YOUR VIEW IS NOT PREDILECTED RIGID OVERT BIAS
2) MAKE SURE YOU ARE NOT GREEDY ON YOUR VIEW
3) MAKE SURE YOU ARE NOT EXITING OUT OF FEAR
4) MAKE SURE YOU ARE NOT ENTERING IN NON TRENDY ZONE OUT OF FOMO
5) MAKE SURE YOU ARE NOT OVER EXCITED OVER CONFIDENT
6) MAKE SURE YOU ARE PLAYING WITHIN MONEY MANAGEMENT WITH RESPECT TO PROFIT WALL
7) MAKE SURE YOU ARE NOT TAKING UNDUE RISK OUT OF MACHO CHARACTERISTIC
8) MAKE SURE YOUR VIEW ACCOMPANIED WITH CHART.

We need to have a trading mindset to become profitable traders. What does it mean? How we can elaborate it.

Trading mindset is the state of mind where we are able to penetrate the market as it's in reality without any emotional dilemma.

Yes . That state of mind will come to your journey too. Time may vary. But if somebody is dedicated and passionate about this art and skill anyone can become a profitable trader.

PREMATURE ENTRIES MENTALITY

1) CHEAP BUYING TENDENCY.
2) FOMO GREED TENDENCY.
3) TRUST DEFICIT ON UNDERSTANDING.
4) UNCONTROLLED BEHAVIOUR.
5) FAILED TO RECOGNISE PATTERN AND RANGE.
6) CLINCHING TO CATCH A TO Z MOVEMENT.
7) NOT WAITING FOR ENOUGH TIME PRICE CORRECTION TILL CROSS OVER.
8) PATIENCE IS ASSET FOR IMPLENTATION.

Cheap buying tendency is one of the major reasons why we encounter loss in the trading.

Just because the market offers something at a low price it doesn't mean it's a good opportunity to make money. First choose the right direction then right signal. Whatever the price then it may be a good deal for us.

Remember healthy trade comes at a healthy price . Fear of missing out leads us to take premature entries without a signal .

As range can vary in the market that tendency can lead us to enter a whole lot of time at wrong places and we encounter big losses.

Just by waiting for a signal to occur we can avoid such silly mistakes to protect our capital and subsequent deterioration.

Don't try to catch a to z movement by predicting top bottom mentality instead entering after confirmation can make you a better trader with overall better results than any such random outcome .

Remember we are here to trade here life time . One day wonder is not going to make you rich.

First calm down your mind with this thought: we are here to trade for a life .

Remove this hurry element in you . Rest your mind has enough potential to tackle the market.

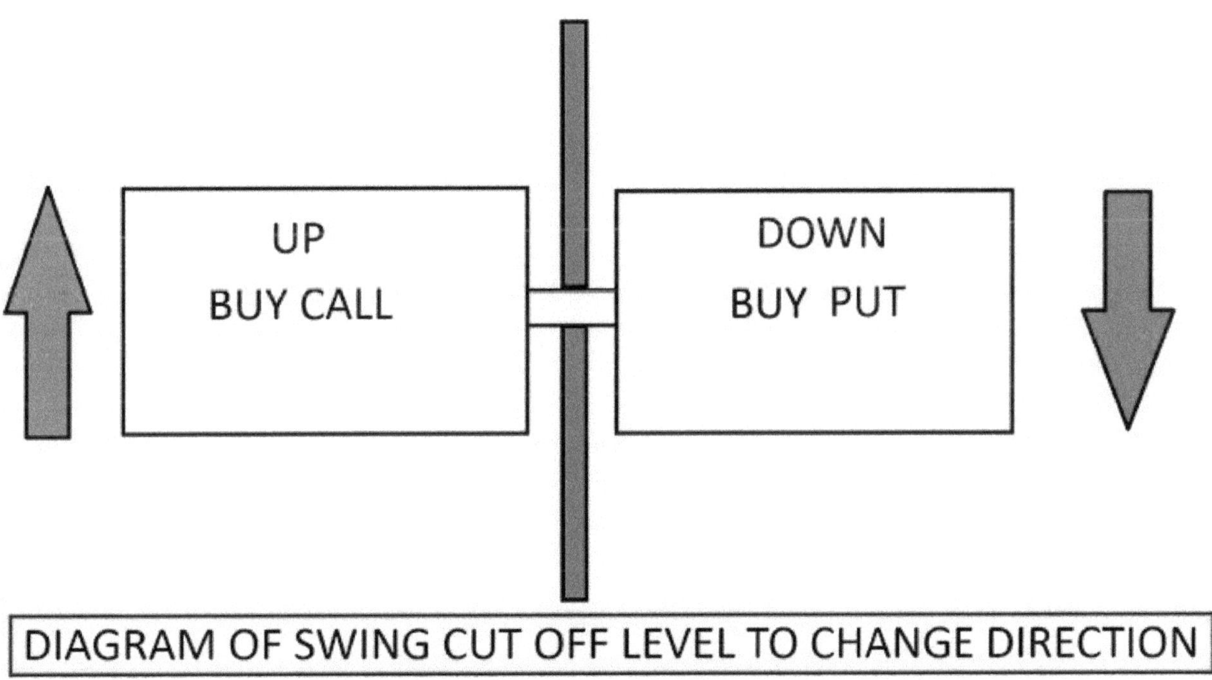

DIAGRAM OF SWING CUT OFF LEVEL TO CHANGE DIRECTION

These are some of the common mistakes we traders perform during our initial years. Which sounds foolish now.

But these things happen. We keep making the same mistake again and again. Our minds get hacked by our primitiveness.

We are no more in our control. Every trader goes through such addictive impulsive hell before they start their profitable journey. We became clueless about what's happening to us.

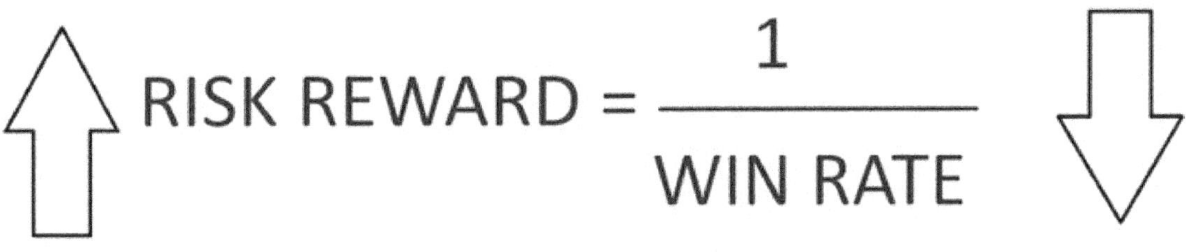

CONTEXT MOMENTUM BASE RISK REWARD.

1) 1 : 1 SLOW SLUGGISH RANGE BOUND MOMENTUM.
2) 1 : 2 OR 1 : 3 NORMAL DAYS ROUTINE MOMENTUM.
3) 1 : 4 : 5 : 6 TRENDY DAYS. MAJOR BREAKOUT PULLBACK REVERSAL. FIRST PULLBACK CONTINUTION ; STRONG 9 EMA TREND ; STRONG B CONTINUTION ; STRONG M W REVERSALS.

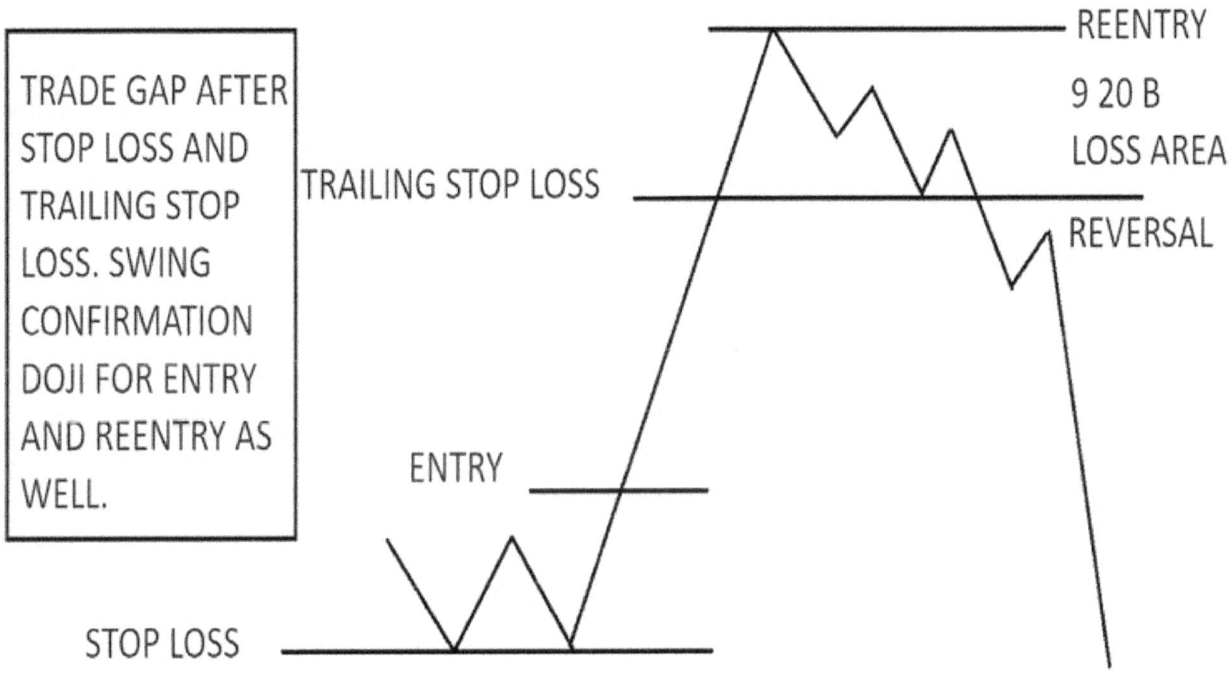

DIAGRAM SHOWING DISTANT REVERSAL WITH PREMATURE REENTRY 9 20 B AREA

Chapter 10

MENTAL CHAOS

So many voices are there as we are living in a digital world. During the early history of the market there was a lack of information but nowadays we are overloaded with it.

To gather all kinds of information scrutiny it testifies its importance and drawbacks, putting it in a sequential manner which can be helpful to us. Required lot of effort and time .

Different traders talk about different approaches, set up strategy, their own entry exit and profit booking ideas that create a whole lot of Chaos in beginners minds.

And the most dangerous part is that unless you follow one approach throughout or be able to apply all of it as per requirement none of these are going to be productive for you. And you remain quite frustrated losing traders for a long time.

For beginners it's very difficult to understand and pursue the very essence of suggestions given by any professional trader. Hence though many people started their journey with coaching classes not able to produce profitable results equivocally.

What they say and what we understand could have a hell lot of difference. A very well known dilemma about profit booking in trading is between risk reward or win rate.

What I learn from my experience is that it all depends upon your level of understanding of price action. If you understand the market with all its variation direction range then you can probably book profit at the right level often.

But for the beginners the same thing is not possible hence the risk reward method of profit booking is useful for them till they gather enough experience to decide range in every trade accurately.

BIASES FACED IN MARKET

1) PULLBACK OR REVERSAL 9 20 B OR M W
2) PERIODICITY BIAS
3) RECENCY BIAS
4) TRAILING OR FIXED RISK REWARD BIAS
5) MOMENTUM OR RR BIAS
6) NO OF TRADES BIAS
7) INDEX BIAS
8) QUANTITY BIAS
9) STOP AND REVERSE BIAS
10) TIME FRAME BIAS
11) MORNING TRADE BIAS
12) DOWNWARD BIAS

TECHNICAL
METHODOLOGICAL
STATISTICAL
BIASES

Mental chaos ought to occur because every new information is half knowledge for us unless we get complete information and absorb it for a long period of time.

And with every upcoming information we try to disregard our current information as we aren't yet profitable traders hence we keep shifting from this strategy to that strategy from this method to that method of profit booking.

For different entry exit signals. For different risk rewards ratios. For different degrees of accuracy what not.

We failed to understand the fact that our mind required much more time to configure trading and synchronised it for implementation. Merely adding more and more information won't help.

Time has no replacement. Trading might take much more time than you anticipate to acclimate it properly.

So be patient and trust the process. It is just like how new learning drivers keep asking repeatedly what to do first in which order instead accepting the fact everything needed to be done simultaneously. But eventually most people are able to drive a car without not much fuss.

Unfortunately the same is not the case with trading. Not many people are able to make simultaneous decisions and adapt according to market situations. They stuck with different individual isolated strategies, sometimes time kept it changing and what not.

They probably can't wait till their synchronisation of learning to occur. In order to complete their knowledge cycle.

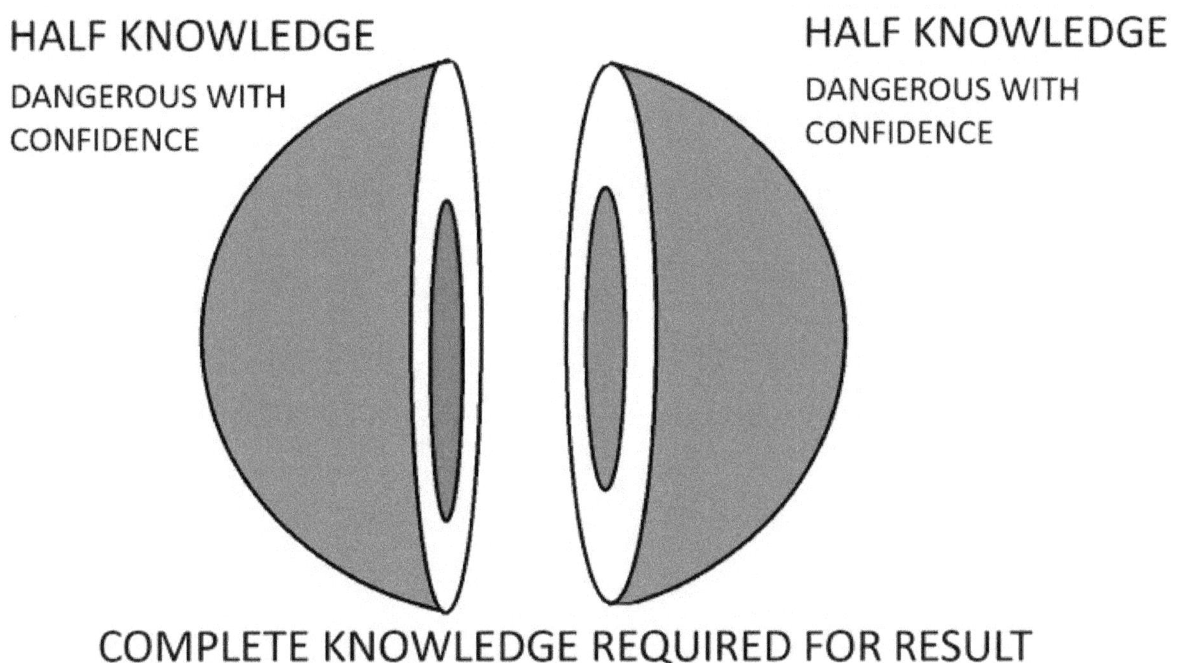

DESPITE HITTING STOP LOSS REPEATADELY ENTERING IN MARKET WITHOUT CONFIRMATION IS EGO BEHAVIOUR IN MARKET.
FIRST TRADE WITHOUT SWING CONFIRMATION IS EGO IN MARKET.

Chapter 11

FIGHT WITHIN

Trading is not just about making money it's more about exploring our own evils within. This fundamentally makes it a distinguished field than rest of the worldly ways of making money.

We hardly know how to introspect ourselves in any field for any kind of progress. Certainly not as much as required in trading for sure. Because we have to fight with our own emotions, premature ideas, misconceptions etc etc.

As I said earlier, trading requires time to learn. It's not a skill which you can learn in a very short period of time with significant depth to pass out. Like in our academics where even you know 50 to 60 % of your due syllabus and you passed out.

No it's not possible in this case. Unless you follow 100 % of your plan, strategy,approach, discipline, concept, context you won't make it as a profitable trader.

That's why probably many people failed in this field. No casual careless approach gives you desired results. Many professionals who are successful in their respective fields may not be successful in trading with the same intensity. This is all together different games .

Required mental adaptation. A delicate state of mind where you can crack market mood every day and day out. It's just like an exam every day.

How do you feel when you come to know you don't have any final exam to accomplish instead every day exam throughout your life. Intraday trading is just like that.

You won't get anything out of a good performance in one day. Series , period, era of discipline required to make something substantial out of it. Which you can cherish for life.

So friends know the seriousness of this business. Probably one of the most difficult skills to pursue on the planet. Accept that trading is not rocket science. But it's the same degree of art to pursue considering the immense emotional hurdles it brings with it.

1) REPEATATION OF PATTERN.
2) INCREASED CLARITY.
3) CONFIRMATION OF SIGNAL.
4) INCREASED MENTAL STABILITY.
5) INCREASED CONSISTENCY.

Settling of mindset is key for implementation. As we know we can't see clearly in boiling water. The same sort of mechanism occurs in trading with boiling emotions; we can't observe market reality.

Market makes you humble and changes your very core . Market makes you realise that yes you can be wrong . You are a highly potential candidate who can be wrong in his understanding .

Wrong in thought process logic concept . You need more time to learn than you think of yourself.

Market realises that you are human with potential for misconception, misinterpretation and mismanagement .

The market teaches you that you can't be perfect. You are just human.

THINGS TO AVOID FOR BETTER SHARP CONSISTENT TRADING

1) CARRY FORWARD TRADE.

2) EXPIRY TRADE IN DISTANT STRIKE PRICE THATS HERO ZERO TRADE.

3) FIRST HOUR TRADING.

4) ACTING ON PRESUMPTIVE STRUCTURE RANGE WITHOUT SIGNAL IN 5 MT CHART. RANGE MAY VARY.

5) PREMATURE EXITS.

Time will come when you realise despite knowing all kinds of price action and all kinds of efforts you are not able to make money due to this or that reason.

Honesty is required in that case. You know everything in the market. Everything on the chart you know what is happening and why despite that you don't choose the right direction.

How did that happen ? What can be a solution for this than your own honesty, your own commitment for betterment of yourself.

Our ego never wants to improve or prove itself wrong in the market. It keepsfighting totakeourselvesinthewrongdirection.

We need to understand this very ego problem of ours. In the market trading is implementation problems not knowing problems .

YOU KNEW IT ALL DONT DO BAIMANI. ITS ALL ABOUT SINCERITY AND HONESTY NOW. DONT WASTE YOUR ATTEMT. TAKE WELL DEFINE REGULAR TRADE. BE AWARE OF ASSUMPTION MANIA EVERY NOW AND THEN.

Despite knowing well defined organised classified price action there is still a possibility you can be on the wrong side of direction and lose money.

Our mind gets frustrated with repetition of mistakes. Time to develop the ability of implementation is always much more than time for knowing the concept here.

The calm down of mind and proper execution occurs quite late. Many people can give up at this stage of their journey because despite all kinds of their efforts results are not visible. And that's quite frustrating.

FIRMNESS.
GRIP.
CONTROL.
DECISION MAKING.
PROMT BOLD SHARP.
LOGIC CONTEXT THEME.

TRADING AN ART OF MAKING MONEY WITH LOGIC AND MATH.

More truly trading is art rather than science. A better trader should be a fantastic artist. He is supposed to know what to do at what point of time.

Trading means timing the market. It could be for a week for a day or for an hour may be for Intraday purpose.

Trader has the quality of managing his risk and taking advantage of market movement opportunities to make multi fold profit of his risk in order to become profitable trader.

ALIGNMENT WITH MOMENTUM

ALIGNMENT WITH CONTRACTION EXPANSION CYCLE

ALIGNMENT WITH DAILY CHART STRUCTURAL FORMATION COMPLETION EXHAUSTION AND STRUCTURAL BREAK.

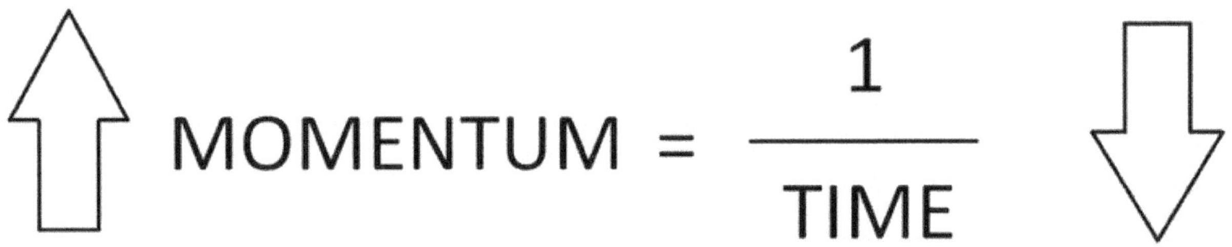

BIG MOVE = BREAKOUT + PULLBACK IN CONTINUTION

Chapter 12

ROLE OF TECHNICAL ANALYSIS

Learning about the share market and trading in it. What does it mean? What are we supposed to learn? What does it contain? What's its syllabus?

Often Beginners are poured with this kind of thousand of questions. Because everyone wants to make as much money as possible as quickly as possible. Our very attachment to money and its correlation with our socioeconomic status and success make us keen to make money.

As money gets tremendous importance in our lives and we all are flooded with our own superiority complexes within our mind and imagination due to ego. We consider ourselves a special entity which can quickly interpret the market in no time and start making infinite money.

Stop, take a pause, take a breath. Things aren't that easy. It wasn't before, it's not now either. Because humans remain the same bunch of emotions with flooded fear, greed, fomo, hope, revenge, anger, and whatnot.

Technical analysis consists of plenty of tools from simple price action to complicated several indicators. But the basic concept remains the same: prediction of the next market move on the basis of past and ongoing scenarios with the help of support resistance , chart pattern , trend line EMA ,sma ,adx ,rsi and plenty more.

In quick summary of technical analysis, the Market can be broadly classified into 2 types.

Uptrend and downtrend. If you are able to identify market structure on a chart with the help of multiple time frame analysis your half job is done. Simple approach of buy on dip in uptrend and sell on rise in downtrend. Can minimise your plenty of hustle.

It sounds so easy. Isn't it. But for practical implementation of it our mind can take several years. Trading concepts are easily aligned with trends but our mind always tends to play opposite to it due to primitive reasons discussed above hence trouble occurs.

And markets are inherently such volatile and dynamic entities. Conquering the mind and keeping it cool and calm in such scenarios is the major challenge in trading. Nevertheless nothing is impossible.

Trading is not an excuse. It's a time consuming journey due to the requirement of mental adaptation.

Pouring plenty of money before your mind gets aligned with the market can only lead to disaster only in the form of severe losses which can be life threatening in many cases. As intraday trading is prone to develop an addictive state of mind. Where wrong habitual pattern formation can spoil you emotionally mentally and economically.

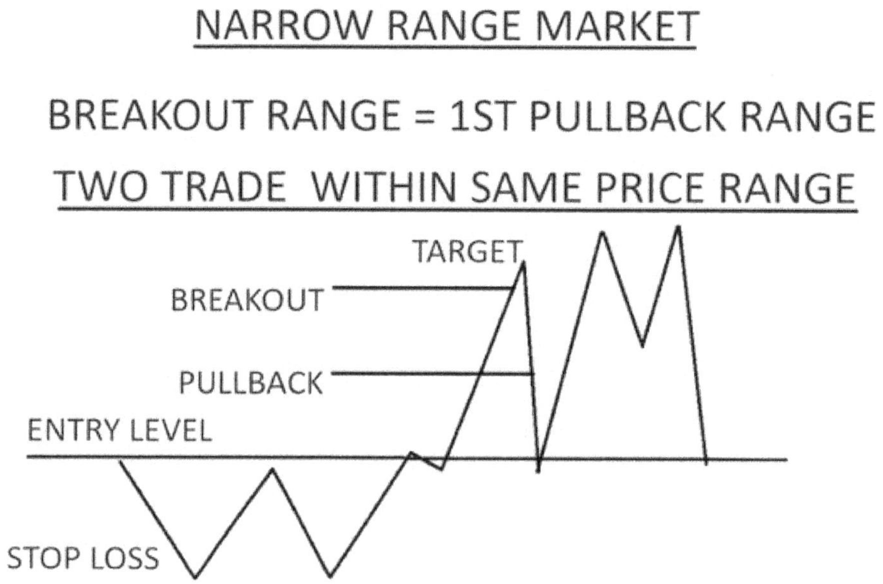

NARROW RANGE MARKET

BREAKOUT RANGE = 1ST PULLBACK RANGE

TWO TRADE WITHIN SAME PRICE RANGE

TARGET
BREAKOUT
PULLBACK
ENTRY LEVEL
STOP LOSS

Most common swing completion w strategy. Have patience to wait for this signal on your chart.

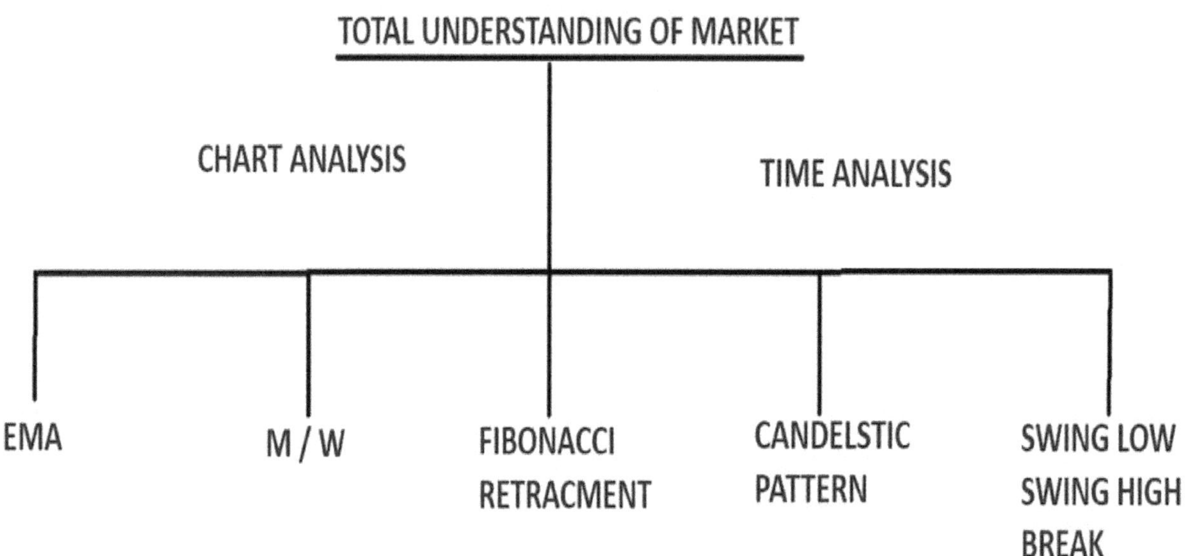

Chart is made up of two things: price on y axis and time on x axis . We need to figure out the cross section point of both price and time on the chart for better entry level.

To figure out that we have many method strategy tools available. It's up to us to decide what suits us most according to our experience on that particular tool as per our approach and trading style.

Its trader state of mind which decides the utility of any tool, strategy not that tool or strategy only.

This is the life cycle of your trade regardless of direction. Trade consists of 3 elements. Stop loss point , entry point and target point.

Our whole aim is to identify such 3 key levels on the chart according to our desired anticipated , planned , direction in order to make profit.

More often we predict these 3 levels and direction right we make money. And the series continues.

Candlestick pattern and chart pattern are important aspects of trading. There are signal double and triple candlestick patterns as well. Which are visible on different time frames of the chart.

Chart pattern is made up of a bunch of candles. A bunch of candle formation occurs in the time correction zone. Breaking of such areas can provide potential direction of the trade. Some of the common patterns include

1) Reversal chart pattern

   M double top bearish signal ;

   W double bottom bullish signal

Head and shoulder;

Inverted head and shoulder

2) Continuation pattern

   Like flags and rectangles.

   Bearish and bullish continuation.

3) Neutral pattern

   Triangle and wedges are neutral patterns depending upon their direction of break.

Simplistic approach to classified intraday move in day trading by using 20 EMA In 15 minute Chart.

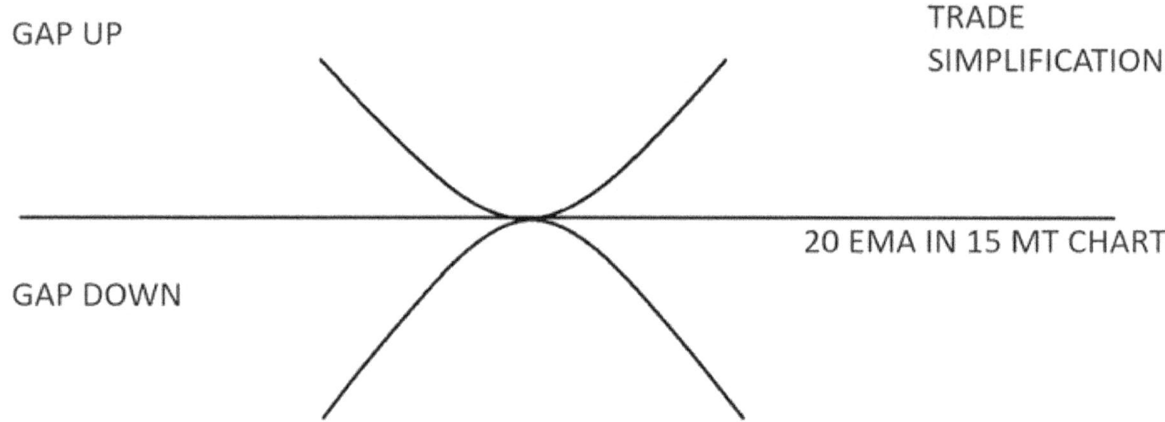

CANDLESTICK PATTERN ALONG WITH SWING COMPLETION DOJI CANDLE ON 15MT CHART IS OUR ENTRY CANDLE. WATCH FOR SUPPORT RESISTANCE BREAK.

This is one of my favourite strategies where we can simply bifurcate trade on up and downside on the basis of 20 EMA in a 15 minute chart.

If the price is above it then it is likely to move further above and if it's down to it it is likely to move further down. Obviously trading is not always that easy.

We need to use this concept according to market underline trends. Reversal can happen across the EMA if there is a strong up or down trend going on in the market.

All that you can distinguish with your experience only. Hence give time to market friends and give time to yourself also to your mind in order to handle variation in the market.

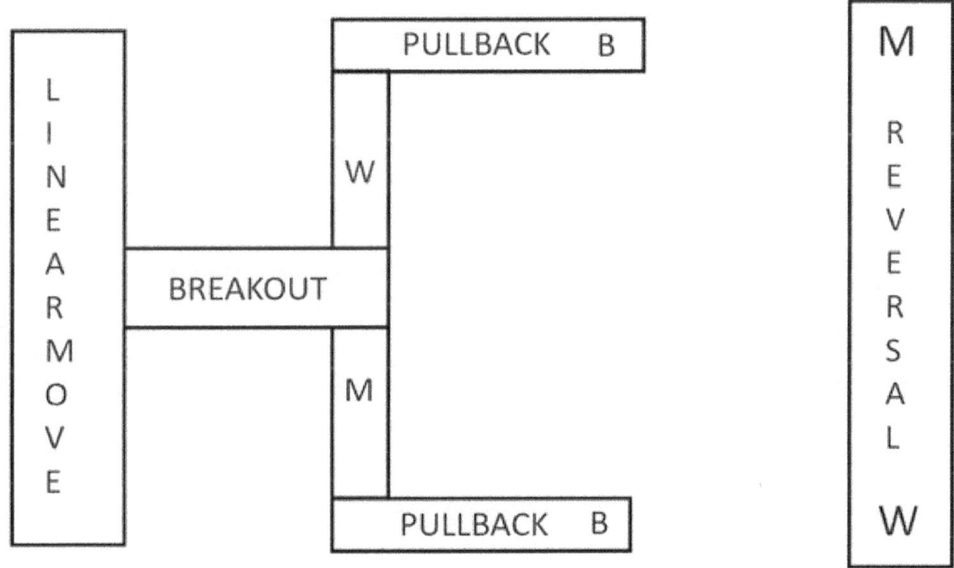

INTRADAY CHART STRUCTURE ALONG WITH FEELING TO DISCRETE TRADE AND RANGE

This is what I found with all my experience for day trading Intraday moves can be broadly classified in the above structure.

Certainly you need to observe these things in the chart over the period of time then you can relate with these diagrams. For that you need to go through this book over and over again.

Trades can be broadly classified into 3 types

1)BREAKOUT

2) PULLBACK

3) REVERSALS

In any time frame trades can be distinguished between the above 3 types. We need to pick up the trade according to the ongoing market scenario as per our trading style which is found very beneficial to us according to our experience profit loss statistics.

We can simply divide every up move as a W and down move as M.

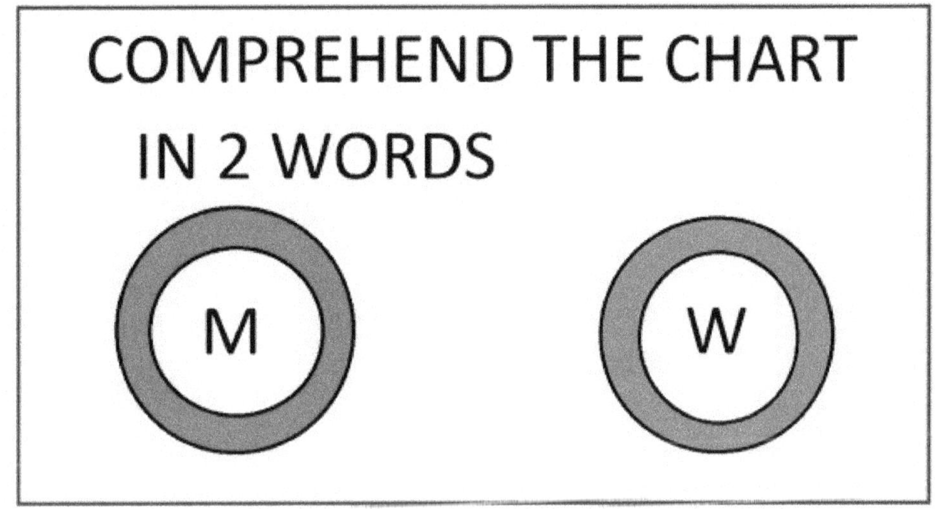

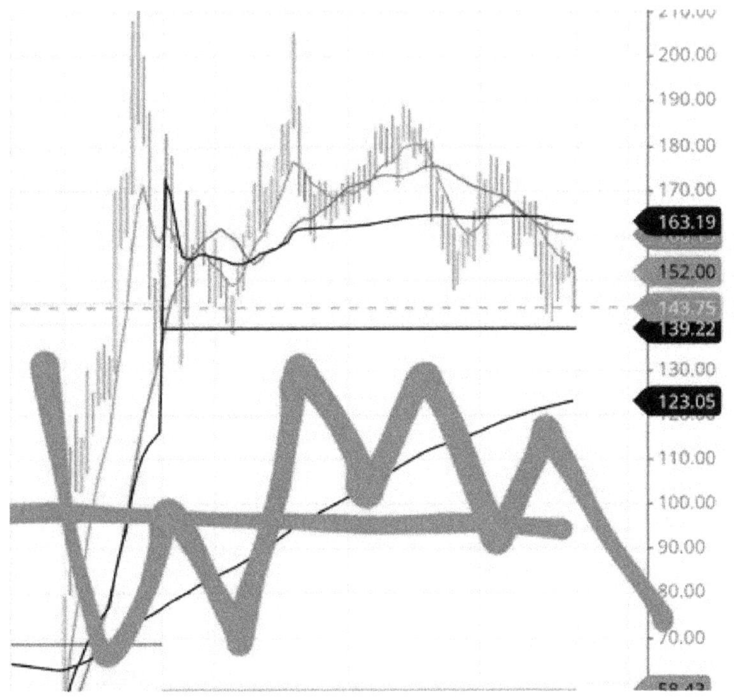

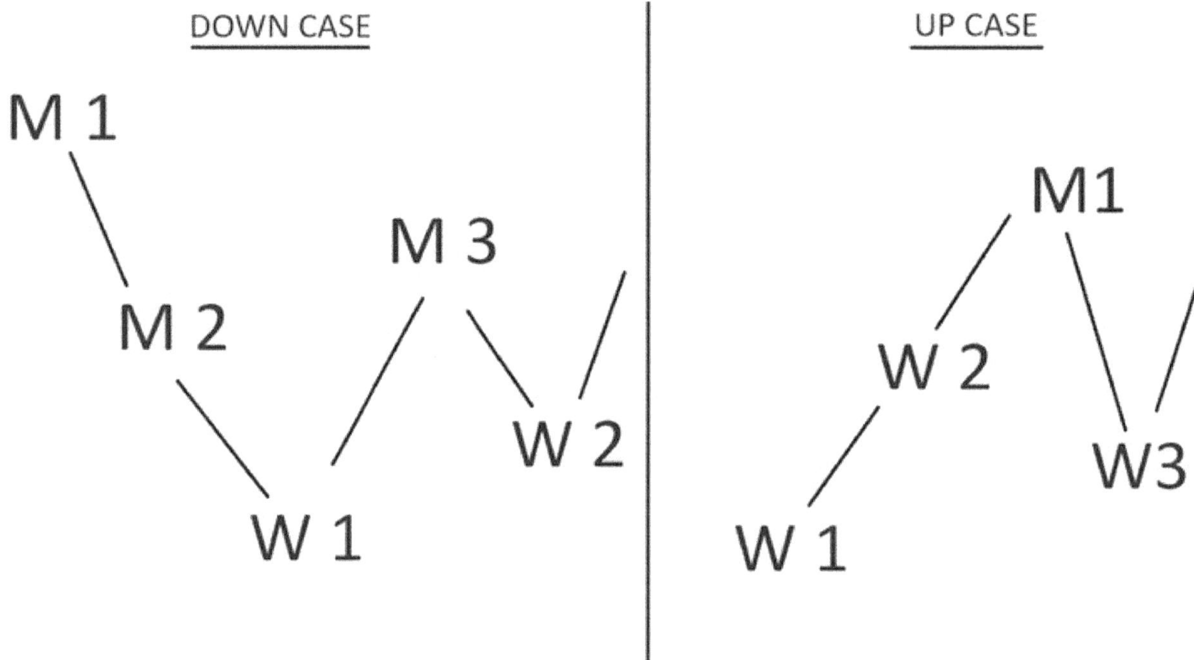

How I approach the chart for day trading. My strategy accompanied two principal orientation approaches. That's the continuation and reversal approach.

I prefer 9 EMA 20 EMA AND B below the EMA concept for continuation purposes. And M W strategy for reversal purpose.

I divide my Trade in two categories 9 20 B which is a continuation concept for me.

And M W that's the reversal component.

Combination of these two approaches gives me better results.

Obviously we need to know overall market structure and sentiment to know which strategy to put continuation or reversals and what part of the day first half and second half.

M W classification according to range

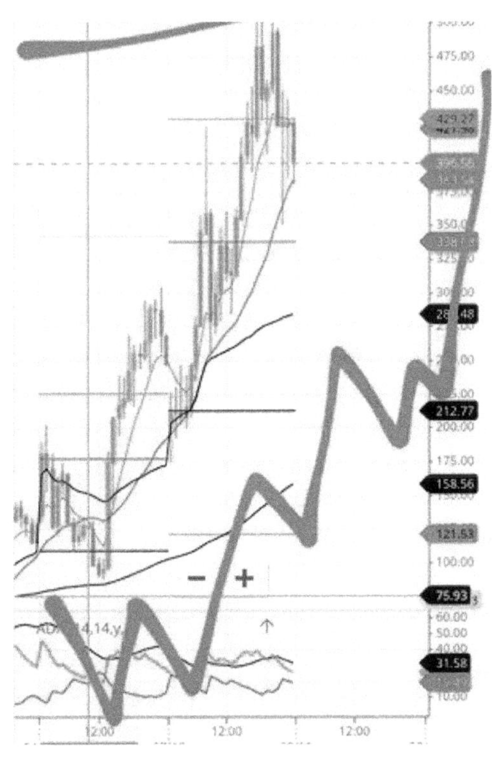

1) Routine M W.

   Normal day range

2) Horizontal MW

   Choppy market

3) Vertical M W

   Big range move both sides

4) Wide M W

   Breakout in second half

	9.15AM TO 11.30AM	11.30AM TO 1.30PM	1.30PM TO 3.30PM
1)	C	C	C 9
2)	R	C	C 20
3)	R	R	C B
4)	R	R	R M/W

C = CONTINUATION , R = REVERSAL

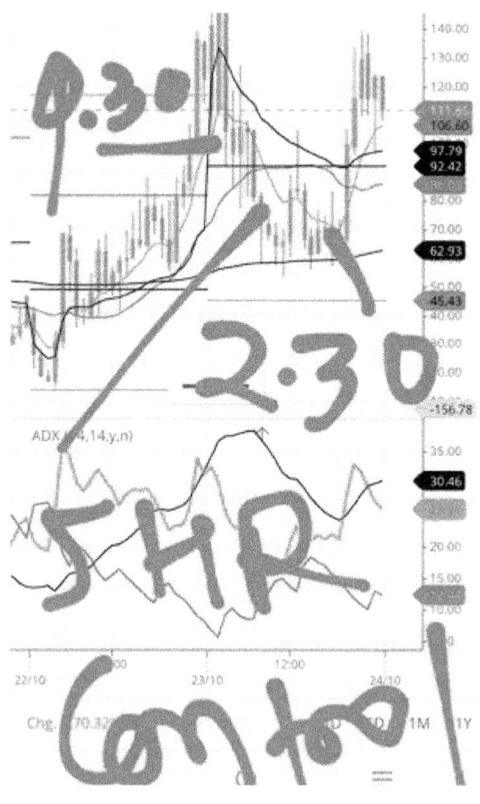

Diagram depicting ema bifurcation of trade .

TREND SENTIMENT TRADE SELECTION

ABOVE AND BELOW 20 EMA OF 15 MT CHART WHICH OF THE FOLLOWING TRADE YOU LIKE TO TAKE FOR BETTER RISK REWARD.

1) BREAKOUT M W	BUY (CONTINUTION)
2) PULLBACK M W	0 1 2 3
3) REVERSAL M W	FREE (REVERSALS)

Multiple time frame analysis is an important aspect of technical analysis to figure out the broader structure of the market of the chart.

Synchronisation of candle formation in all the time frame can give a better idea of Intraday price action creation with an important level in the hand.

Use of technical analysis is to predict the next market move but we are not supposed to entirely depend upon prediction. Instead we need to observe first some kind of evidence on the chart which gets aligned with our prediction.

Technical analysis provides us a better entry point in the market with proper stop loss and target level. Certainly good technical analysis skill and experience of market sentiment with momentum base reward policy can put you ahead in this game.

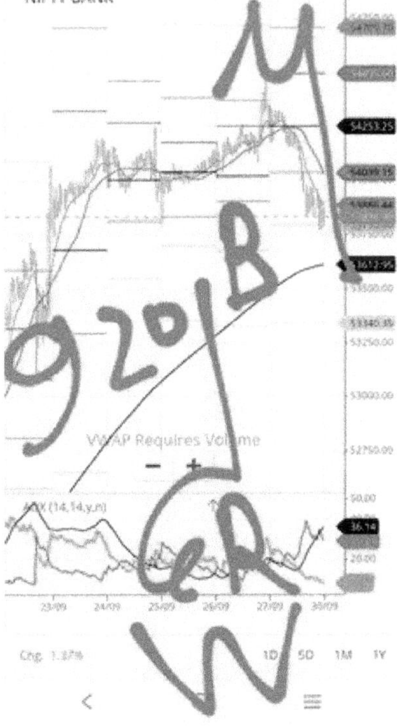

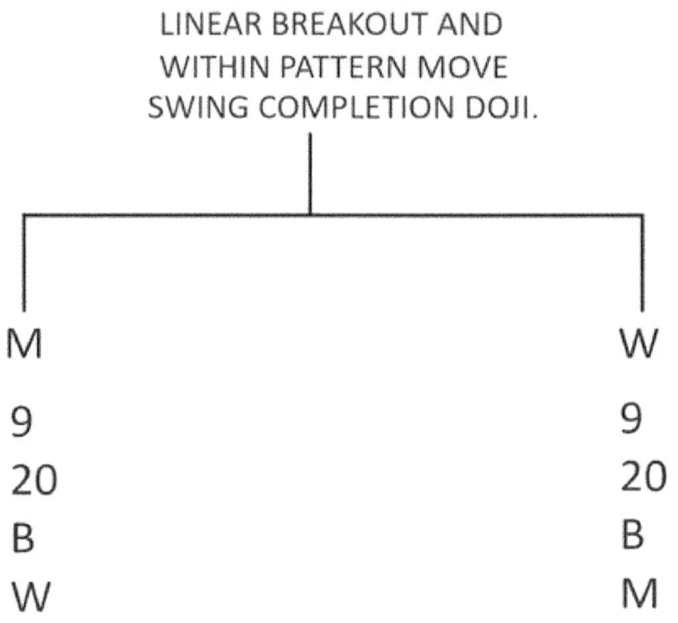

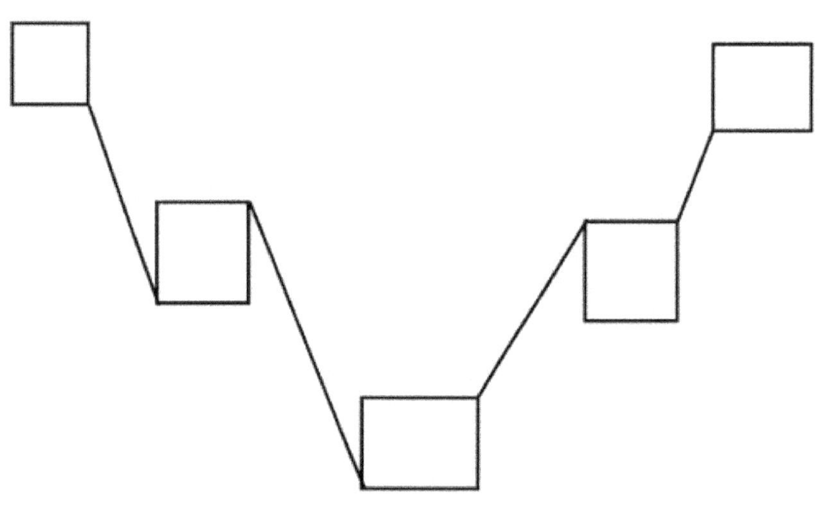

WHICH 5 MT BOX TO PLAY

Chapter 13

TRADING MATHS

We need to understand the difference between stop loss and loss. Loss could be huge if you aren't abiding to planned trade according to your level.

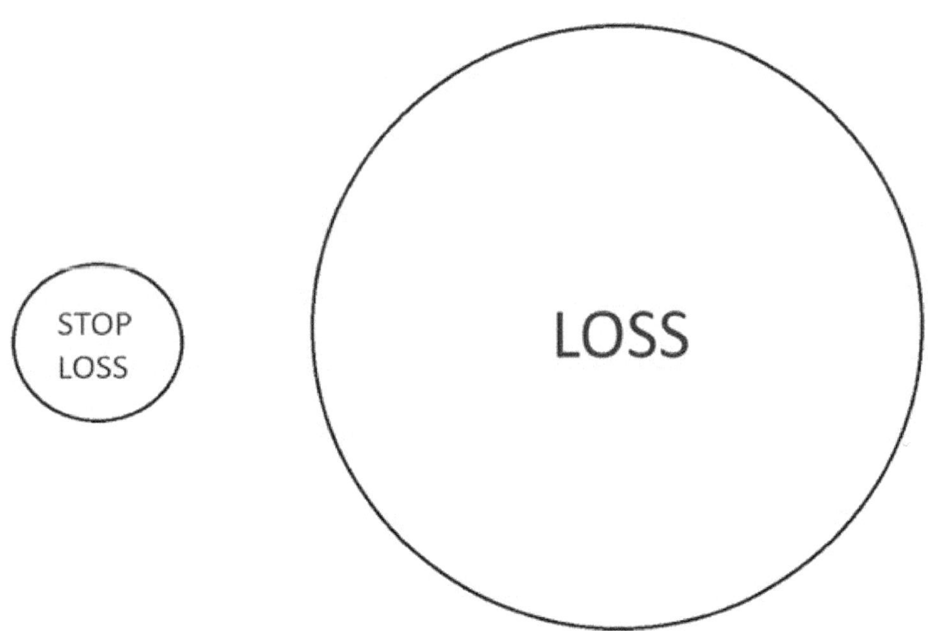

What are the causes of excessive losses in Intraday trading.? Lack of logical concept behind the trade. Overtrading in the same direction. Despite the market giving signals to stop and reverse.

Time price analysis needs to be done prior to entry set up. Opportunities are scattered present in the market. On some days full of opportunities while on another day nothing. Ability to distinguish between opportunities and utilising most of it need mental temperament.

Quick adaptation according to market overall gyration and according to Intraday momentum price action. Often your trading decisions are right, it's obvious for you to remain in profit.

Cap upper limit of your loss in Intraday. Profit can vary according to the situation. Try to make 60 to 70 percent of the day profitable. That will provide sustainability to you in the market without major drawdown. And your loss limit should be half of your daily average profit.

If your daily average profit is 15k to 20k Then you shouldn't lose anything more than 8k to 10 k in Intraday whatever case.

Money management is an important aspect of trading. Without it profitability is not possible. Surviving in the market with our capital is the challenging task in initial years.

Major culprit of capital deterioration is our big losses caused due to over-trading when we don't get reversed and aligned with the market due to our ego stupidity and rigidity.

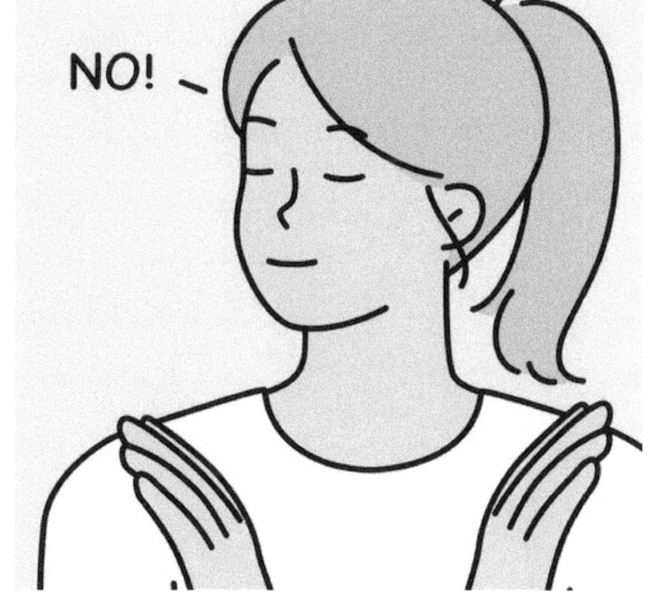

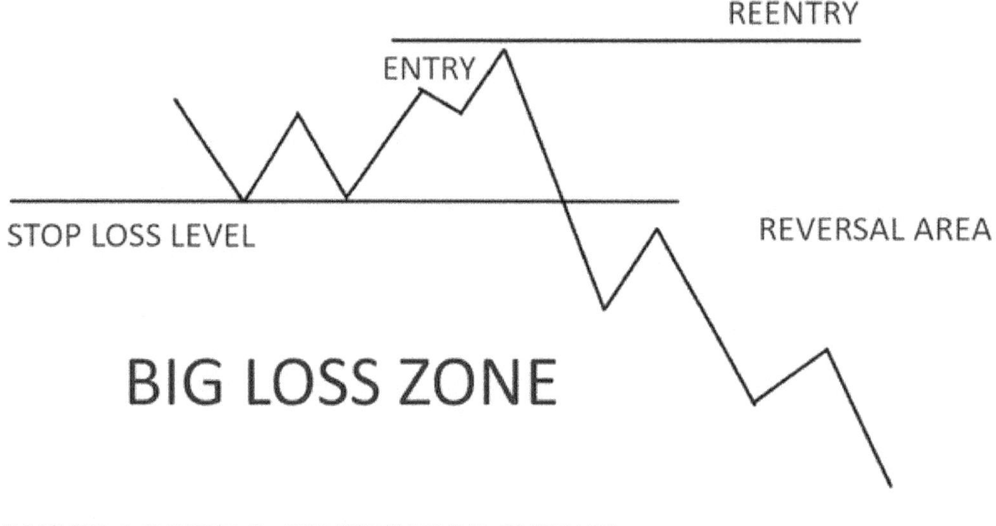

Another emotional block that occurs in trading is when we take any trade in the morning either up or down.

Say upside if you randomly took a trade for upside and market got reversed we keep trying to take a trade for upside despite our stop loss got hit and our screen shows loss.

We experience a sort of panic reaction due to loss on our screen. In order to recover the loss we try to play an impulsive and absurd manner in the same direction of our morning trade.

Instead noticing and acknowledging that the market got reversed from here.

And we need to place positions according to market direction which is downside in this case.

Such a kind of idiotic behaviour we often perform in the market we encounter big losses while doing so and our profit loss statement never improves. We need to fix this behaviour.

COMMON SENSE MATTERS

1) BIG LOSSES CEASES THE POSSIBILITY OF PROFITABALITY.
2) MONEY MANAGEMENT IS THE KEY TO SUCCESS REGARDLESS OF YOUR SET UP WHETHER PULLBACK OR REVERSAL OR YOUR SELECTION OF EITHER IN LIVE MARKET.
3) REGARDLESS OF TIME FRAME REACTIONARY LEVEL DOESNT CHANGE IN INTRADAY TRADING.
4) PROXIMAL DISTAL DISTANT REVERSAL APPROCH COULD HELP YOU RECTIFY WEAK SIGNAL ON 5 MT CHART.
5) WE HAVE TO TAKE ONLY THOSE 5 MT SINGAL WHICH ARE ALIGNED WITH 15 MT CHART VIEW.

Overtrading is one of the major culprits behind why most of the traders are not profitable. First trade loss can elicit a vicious cycle of overtrading.Toavoidovertradingweneedtohaveourownwelltested strategy . Our logical confidence and trust over it can make us profitable.

Most traders fall victim of overtrading which turns their p and l statement red due to big loss in between. Big loss is a big problem and the major cause of it is nothing but overtrading.

Try to figure out your reason behind your trading to fix your overtrading problem. Without fixing it your trading journey won't improve. Figure it out cause its technical psychological emotional method related or what.

To stop over trading one can adapt to fix one or two trade per day policy.

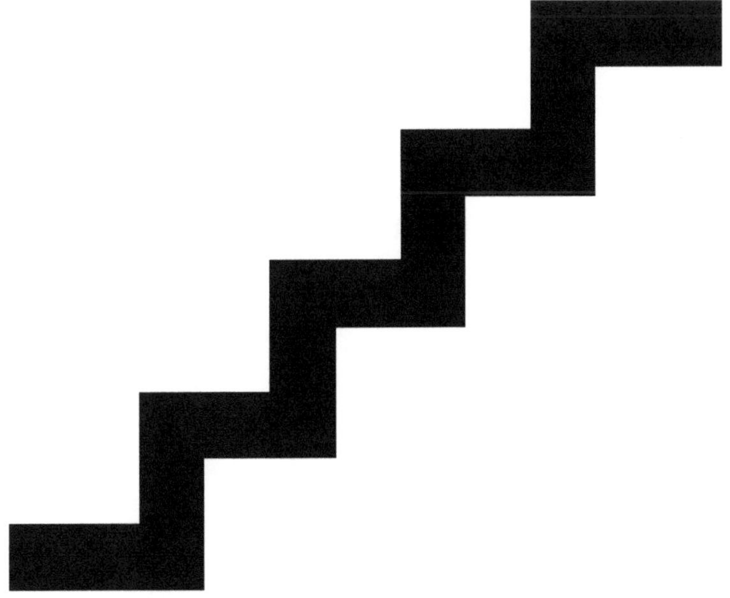

1) INCREASED QUANTITY DOESNT MEAN INCREASED DAILY LOSS LIMIT.
2) SMALL QUANTITY DOESNT MEAN ACTING ON PREMATURE SIGNALS.
3) YOU ARE UNNECESSARY WASTING 200 POINTS OF MAX QUANTITY DUE TO OVERTRADING . THIS IS YOU NEED TO UNDERSATND FIRST. DUE TO STOP LOSS SHIFTING.
4) 29 SECOND PROBLEM. IMPATIENT BEHAVIOUR. AGAINST TREND PLAYING. THIS IS YOUR BIG LOOP HOLE IN YOUR UNDERSTANDING.
5) ACT ON HIGH PROBABILITY SIGNALS PATIENTLY HONESTLY.

HOW TO GROW SMALL DEMAT ACCOUNT ?

To grow a small demat account we need to have our own approximate profit and loss limit that will keep your mind in check.

Making available profits according to market momentum in small quantities can enhance your profit wall with compounding. Don't waste much .

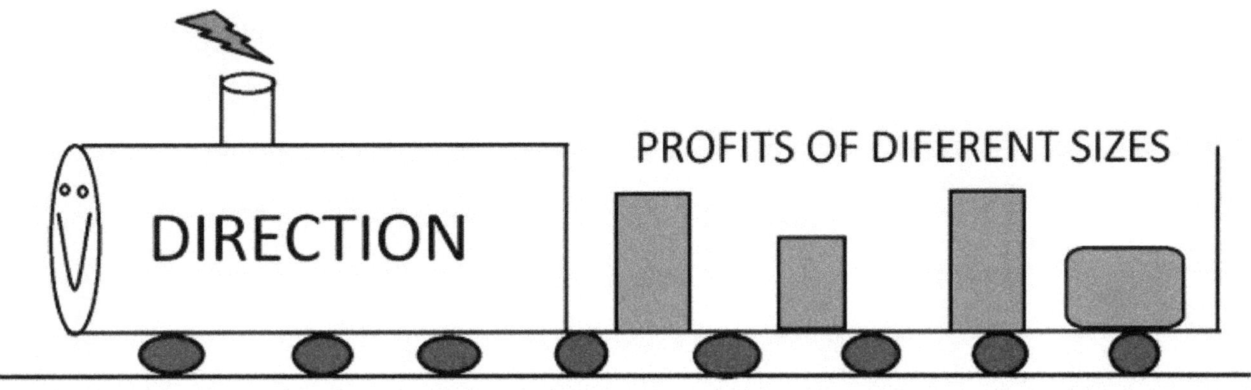

FOCUS ON DIRECTION FIRST. IT`S AN ENGINE FOR OUR PROFITABLE JOURNEY. ACCEPT PROFITS OF DIFFERENT SIZES AND SHAPES FOR COMPOUNDING OF PROFITS.

M/W ITS SUBSEQUENT PULLBACK AND TIMING FOR REVERSAL.

If you have controlled your mind not to lose big your account can easily grow with small medium profits as well.

Don't use a daily loss limit unnecessarily. Protect capital only for the right trade. Take a trade when it's there and book profit as per momentum according to market intraday structure.

Don't go for a fixed target. It can lead to a longer drawdown phase. Use your price action knowledge completely. Turn your knowledge into money . Go for compounding over the period of time step by step.

Don't jump for big profits. Momentum base reward is a good policy to grow a small account. For that you need to have good experience of the chart to feel it but within a logical framework.

And the time gap after morning profit and loss is the most important thing to remember . It's helpful to avoid overtrading and make better decisions.

Starting with a small quantity and then capitalising it gradually this approach suits well to grow a small account.

Small quantity will keep in check your emotions hence you will be able to respond to market momentum and any change in it.

FOCUS ON RIGHT ENTRY

⇩

BETTER STOP LOSS

⇩

BETTER TARGET

Focusing on the right entry can reduce your problem of overtrading. Try to reduce your number of trades by waiting for fulfilment of your trade entry criteria.

This habit can certainly provide better stop loss and target preposition and better results in long term horizon with peace of mind.

PROFIT – LOSS = NET PROFIT

Whole aim of trading art is to create a difference between your profit and loss in order to become a net profitable trader.

You can't completely abolish your losses, you need to reduce it to a minimal level . With all your understanding of price action knowledge experience.

Also Making big profits whenever you get a good set up your liking is also important to create this difference.

You need to conquer this mindset temperament to maximise use of high probability opportunities in the market. That can grow your trading account substantially.

TECHNICAL GLITCH SWING CUT OF LEVEL FOR TURNAROUND M W + MATHEMATICAL GLITCH 200 POINTS DAILY LOSS LIMIT	DONT LOOSE MORE THAN 100 POINTS WHATEVER CASE FOR THAT 2 SL POLICY MUST 1) FIRST TRADE MUST BE GOOD BEST AS PER OVERVIEW 2) SECOND TRADE MUST BE WITH CONFIRMATION TIPS : 2 SL IN ROW NO TRADE

Certainly points and money management aspects are important. That's a good way to monitor our profit and losses. Rather than risking too much capital during initial years try to catch maximum points at the risk of small points. Make sure you don't lose more points than you earn.

BE AWARE ABOUT THE REAL VALUE OF MONEY

+1K > > > -5K -10K -20K -25K -30K
-40K -50K -60K -70K -80K
-100K -120K -140K -160K
-180K

PLEASE UNDERSTAND THE DIFFERENCE BETWEEN THESE VALUE.

Above image is for sensitization of money. This is also one of the mind hacks that occur in trading.

We forget the real value of money on digital platforms. We consider a mere number to it. This is probably one of the reasons why we became reluctant to cut our losses short.

Instead of making 1k 2k profit we can lose multiple thousands despite no trade on the chart . No potential logical trade available.

Hence sensitise your mind for digital representation of the money. No, it's worth it.

TWO TRADE FORMULA TO AVOID PANIC OVERTRADING ATTACK

MORNING	EVENING
1) UP ⇧	1) UP ⇧
2) UP ⇧	2) DOWN ⇩
3) DOWN ⇩	3) DOWN ⇩
4) DOWN ⇩	4) UP ⇧

This is one of the approaches to Intraday trading in which the Intraday market is broadly classified into two halves. Where price movement can be in the same direction in both halves or can go in opposite directions. I call it parallel or Contra Intraday movement.

PREREQUISITE FOR EMOTIONAL STABILITY IN MARKET IS CONCEPTUAL COMPREHENSION OF CHART.
AND APPROACH IN LIFE IN GENERAL. TURTLE APPROACH BENEFICIAL. LONG TERM LIFE TIME GOAL.

IMPORTANT EMOTIONL ATTRIBUTES

1) STILLNESS PATIENCE FOR SELECTION OF TRADE.
2) FIRMNESS GRIP OVER ONCE LEARNED EARNED UNDERSTANDING.
3) IN NON LINEAR ENVIORNMENT CHART FEELING HAS SIGNIFICANT ROLE TO MEET THE REALITY.
4) PURE EMOTIONS CAN PROVIDE EDGE IN MARKET. CHART FEELING WITHOUT FOMO GREED HOPE FEAR ANGER REVENGE EGO. EGO TENDS YOU TO TRADE AGAINST THE DIRECTION OF INTRADAY TREND REPEATEDLY.

Chapter 14

SYNCHRONISATION FOR SUCCESS

No doubt that to become successful in trading we need to have good command over technical analysis, Market structure. Very well orientation of its behaviour, patterns and strategy according to it.

But the power and capacity of learning and implementing all those things lies in the state of mind. Profound struggle happens just to acquire the golden equilibrium of mindset where you are able to implement your knowledge and understanding according to scenario.

The word is synchronisation of all your gathered experience logic concept context timing. Your grip on market sentiment and potential profitable strategy according to it determine the outcome of it. One solo thing not but contribution many things required to become a successful profitable trader.

If you are ready to give enough time to let your mind absorb those concepts without pouring much money during the initial year then you can be a profitable trader in time to come.

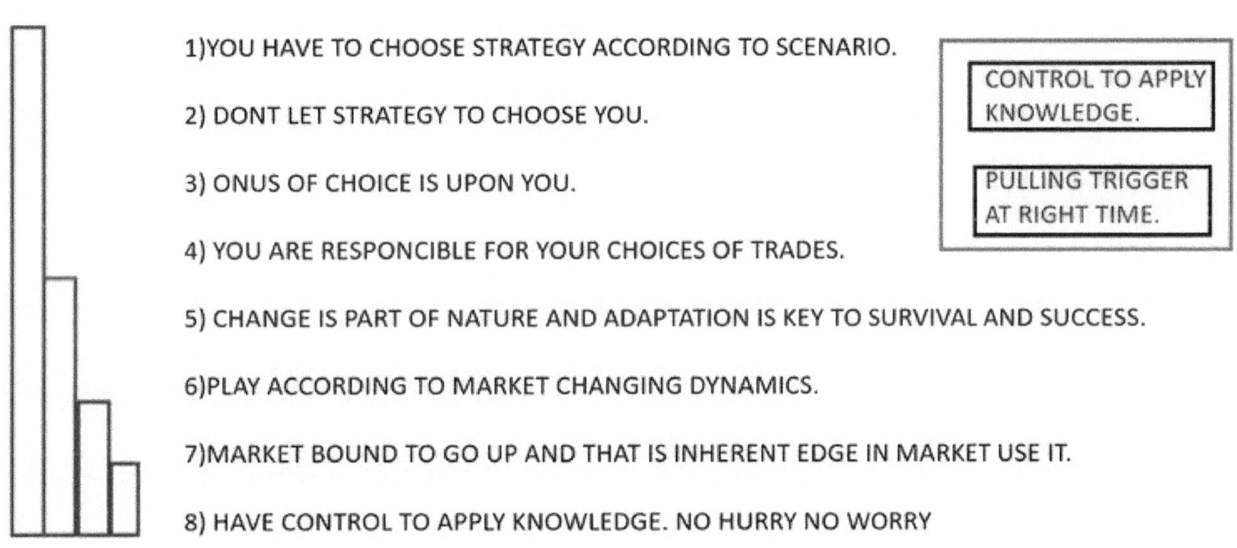

Below image depicted 3 important fundamental blocks for the successful profitable trader. The combination of all 3 required to generate positive results. Even one pillar not working the whole structure may collapse.

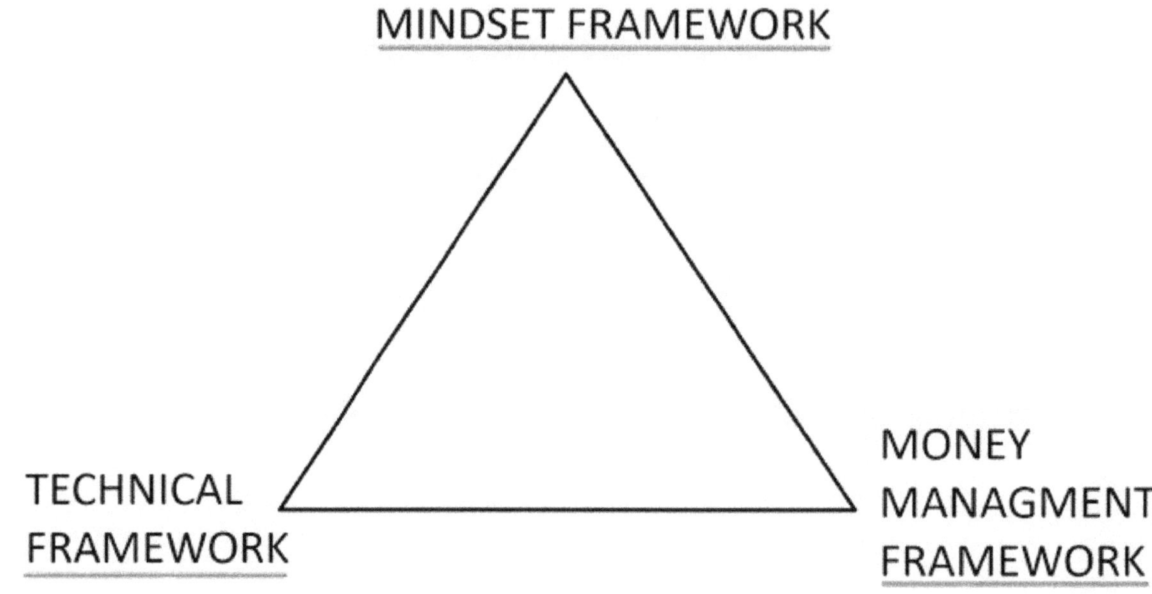

TRADING MIND EVOLUTION FROM YEARS OF LOSSES HUSTLE TO ERA OF LIFE TIME WISDOM PEACE STABILITY PROFITABILITY

1) EMOTIONAL HURDULES IN LEARNING
2) YEARS OF IGNORANCE
3) YEARS OF MISINTERPRETATION MISCONCEPTION
4) YEARS OF LACK OF KNOWLEDGE DISCIPLINE
5) YEARS OF CONTINUE ILLOGICAL LOSSES
6) YEARS OF ADDICTION SAME MISTAKES AGAIN AND AGAIN
7) YEARS OF HAMMERING ON CONFIDENCE
8) EVENTUALLY GRADUAL ONSET OF IMPROVEMENT
9) AFTER YEARS OF GRINDING ERA OF SYNCHRONISATION

PROFIT CONSISITENCY NEW NORMAL NOW DONT MAKE SO MUCH FUSS OUT OF IT

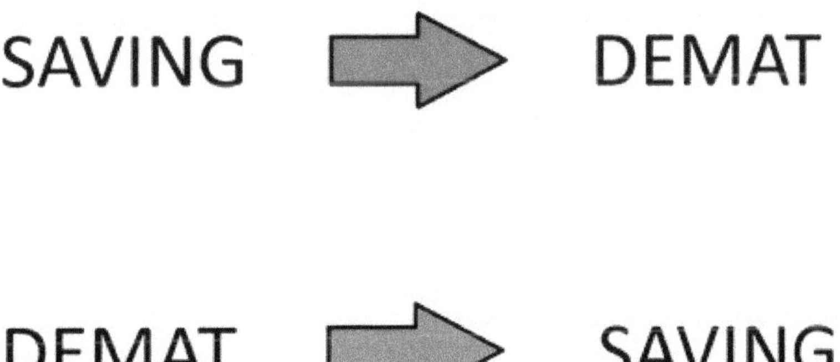

BEHAVIOURAL LOSS
CAN NOT BE
ACCEPTABLE NOW

www.ingramcontent.com/pod-product-compliance
Lightning Source LLC
LaVergne TN
LVHW070935160826
845679LV00021B/1806
* 9 7 9 8 8 9 6 3 2 9 0 1 5 *